MW01680741

Him

~~im~~paired

Him

~~im~~mature

Him

~~im~~part

Him still changes EVERYTHING

Sonny Gann

ISBN: 978-0-9964151-1-8
Library of Congress Control Number: 2016944586
Published in the United States of America

Print History
2024
ISBN: 978-0-9964151-1-8
Cover design – Pati Gann
Edited: Sonny Gann
Library of Congress Control Number:

Dedication

Him Still Changes Everything is dedicated to you, the reader.

In memory of my Mom, Dad, and my sister, Gail: Thank you for being the best family imaginable. I truly miss everything about y'all except for Gail's cooking.

Pati: Thank you for loving me through all things. Thank you for sharing the old things and encouraging me in the new things. You inspire me. And thank you for the journey of Godly marriage. I love you.

Melissa: You are amazing beyond words. Your courage is inspirational. Your fortitude to stay strong in Him provides a glimpse of His grace and mercy! I love you.

Rhonda: Thank you for not giving up on yourself or God. You are indeed a living example of Jeremiah 29:11-13. You now know that God has a plan for you and it is for good. Keep seeking Him and know that you can do all things through Christ who gives you strength. Phil. 4:13 I love you.

Jens and Bill: Thank you for being Godly men. Serving Him well ushers in the ability to serve your family better. I can sleep well at night knowing my girls are cared for. I love you.

The Gannkids... Rylee, Reed, Marielle and Samuel: You are simply awesome beyond awesome. Gannpa loves you.

Contents

Introduction

Improbable as it may seem, here we go again. The improbable has been revealed as undeniably Himprobable. Each Him-word from the first book has truly been lived out in my life as Him Changes Everything has been printed, published, distributed, recorded as an audio book, and offered through Gateway Church (Pulon Press), Amazon, Anchor Distribution, Burkhart Books, ChristianAudio, iTunes, Hoopla, and GoodReads). As I walk with you through the process that leads up to writing the second book, I think it would be fun to share an abbreviated journey of the first book, Him Changes Everything. Just in case you have not read the first book, each word noted below represents a chapter from Him Changes Everything and the definition.

Himpression – *the life-changing effect of living a life that places Him first in thought, relation, emotion, and action.*
Himpact – *life collisions that reflect God's grace and mercy.*
Himpossible – *With God, all things are possible.*
Himprobable – *likely to be true and to happen as God designed*
Himpowered – *confident in the assurance that God gives and delegates power and authority, enables and permits.*
Himbrace – *pressing into the truth of His Word and unfailing love, receiving His grace and mercy*
Himperfect - *God removes defects, weaknesses, and thru Him, all are perfected*
Himposition - *Alignment with God's purpose in your life eliminates the burden and introduces opportunities to have great significance*
Himperative - *Absolutely necessary for God's plan and design to proceed and we should be aware of it*
Himbarrassed - *Putting God first will change your perspective of feeling confusion or self-consciousness*
Himage - *a representation or likeness of a person or thing, especially in scripture*
Himportant - *awareness of God in all things*
Himpatient - *placing Him first removes restlessness*

Himphatic - *unapologetically and lovingly living out the truth of His promises.*

Himmersion - *the "soul" purpose of living a life involved deeply in Him*
Himself - *an emphatic appositive of* **Him,** *redefining yourself as Himself*

For those of you who read Him Changes Everything, and as you now read Him Still Changes Everything, I hope you will be reminded of the powerful and compelling stories skillfully woven into a unique tapestry of linguistic delight and profound intellectual discourse. If you just squinted and reread that sentence, there is a good chance that you actually did read Him Changes Everything and are wondering, "What the heck is he talking about?"! I do hope you read the first book and enjoyed the stories, but most important is that you realize the significance of putting Him first in every aspect of your life and have recognized your own 'Him' stories.

If you are a rule follower and have followed logical progression by reading the first book first, I must ask you to grant a little grace to our non-conforming friends as I feel obligated to share an abridged version of how Him Changes Everything began.

I am a lousy typist/texter (I think I just invented another new word).I mis-typed the word impression by typing Himpression, which caused me to ponder the word Himpression so much I offered it as a prayer for a good friend who was interviewing for a new job. Other words that have the prefix of im- and em- began to occupy my thoughts so I began to make notes and after many many many months a book was birthed. In the first book I also explained the literary significance of repeating a word three times, so don't think you just found a mistake.

As you continue reading, I hope you will recognize a fundamental truth intertwined throughout this book. God loves you! God sent His Son for you. God's Son died for your sin and was resurrected for your eternal salvation. God is not angry with you. God loves you. God pursues you. God's grace is sufficient for you. God's mercy for you is undeniable. No matter where you are as you explore these pages, I pray that the words of this book will humbly, yet miraculously, set in motion a transformation. The sole purpose of Him Still Changes Everything has the same foundational message as Him Changes Everything; the sole purpose of this book is specific to 'soul' purpose. Restated, the one and only purpose of this book is, with Godly intent, to impact who you are in Him.

Positively, one of the most interesting aspects of writing my first book, Him Changes Everything, has been the feedback I received from a variety of people. I love the fact that the feedback revealed an inconsistency of a favorite chapter. Some readers liked the Himpression chapter, some liked Himpossible, many of the guys liked Himpowered, and some folks liked Himbraced. And then there are those who received the book but never commented, and I think I should thank them. I do not handle criticism well! I am assuming (I know I should not) they did not comment for a couple of reasons; they did not read it or they did not like it. Please know I did not write the book to receive affirmation; I wrote the book to share Him, and I have written Him Still Changes Everything to continue to share 'Him'.

It has also been interesting to receive different ideas for other im- and em- words, bible stories and scripture references that seem to be appropriate, or even better than the ones I shared. I actually considered editing the book to include other personal stories and better bible stories to reflect the purpose of the chapter, but it struck me that I would never stop editing. Each and every day offers new relationships, new opportunities, and new revelations of Him that could be added to Him Changes Everything, so I will just leave it as is.

I have been asked several times which chapter was most important to me, and I honestly do not have a favorite chapter. Each chapter represented something different about me and something different about the character of God. Whether the focus was His importance, His image, His patience, His power, His impact, His embrace, or His purpose (emphatic, immersion, improbable, imperative, imposition), every chapter was about Him and my 'self', your 'self', and putting Him first in every aspect of our lives so that we might draw closer and closer to realizing our identity in Him.

And that brings me to this book, Him Still Changes Everything, and the first chapter, Himpaired. I do not want to dissuade you from reading the entire book, but if you can only muster up enough time, energy, and interest, please read Himpaired. Actually, do yourself a favor and do not just read it; meditate on the message, embrace the purpose, and apply the truth to your daily walk.

Chapter 1 Himpaired

Impaired - being in an imperfect or weakened state or condition

Himpaired - an imperfect or weakened state or condition overcome by faith in Jesus Christ

You may be asking, impaired from what? That's a very good question as it sets the premise for the chapter. God's desire is for each of us to be in constant pursuit of our full identity in Jesus Christ. This process begins with an awareness that who we are is consistently reflected by accepting whose we are. The reality is we are impaired in every facet of life beginning with our first breath. As an infant knows from day one, happiness is impaired by their constant need to be fulfilled. Their hunger-screams alert us to the fact their little tummies need to be fully filled. Their tantrum screams alert us to fulfill their need to be attended to, often for no apparent reason. Their 'my-diaper-has-been-fully filled' scream is a plea for mommy to take care of business so daddy doesn't throw up. The infant has a hunger that needs to be fed, a longing to be loved, and a desire to be clean. Ironically, we never really grow out of those basic necessities. The attributes of the necessities may look different as we grow, but we always need to be fed, loved, and clean.

Our minds hunger to be fed with truth. Our souls crave to be clean. Our hearts beat to be loved and to love. Yet, we live our lives daily in a world that tells us that we are just fine where we are, impaired by relationships, false identity, consequences of past choices, anger over an unfair diagnosis, fear over future uncertainties, chaos of guilt, and anxiety laced with desperation. The definition of impaired was stated as, being in an imperfect or weakened state or condition. Yes, we are.

Isaiah 43:18-19 says, But forget all that, it is nothing compared to what I am going to do. For I am about to do something new. See, I have already begun! Do you not see it? I will make a pathway through the wilderness. I will create rivers in the dry wasteland.

I pray as you contemplate this idea, there will be a sense of His presence and you will be moved from impaired to Himpaired; an imperfect or weakened state or condition overcome by faith in Jesus Christ.

I am 6'3" which is typically an advantage. I say typically because my height provides an advantage on the racquetball court, basketball court, movie theatre, at the dinner table (I also have long arms), and seeing over all of you short people at parades and events. However, there are scenarios when I have been impaired by my height. Try sitting in the middle seat on an airplane with a 'leaner' in the seat in front of you. With a 'leaner' in the seat in front of me, my height impairs my ability to achieve a smidgeon of comfort as the leaner crushes my kneecaps.

My Christianity impairs my ability to tell the rude, impolite, disrespectful, knee-cap-crusher exactly what I am thinking about doing to him or her as soon as I get the feeling back in my legs and feet. The situation impairs my ability to enjoy the free beverage because I know for a fact I will be unable to enjoy a leisurely restroom break. Previous attempts to stand after two hours of having my legs numbed has given the appearance I have been sipping a little more than the free drinks. Approximately two hours into an eight-hour flight, and sympathetic to my agony, my sweet bride asked me if I would like to stretch my legs. No sweetheart, I have no desire to stretch my legs! I would actually like to shrink my legs and then play jackhammer on the back of the leaner's seat as he/she tries to take a sip of steaming hot coffee. I feel so much better now. Thank you for letting me vent. Lord forgive me of my desire to be an irritant to the leaner. (If you are a leaner…repent!)

I considered making a list of all of the impaired people in the Bible, but I was quick to realize that would be silly. The Bible provides a very long list of impaired people; people who are imperfect or in a weakened state or condition.

I thought it would be interesting to open the bible to a random page and use the main character of the first scripture on the left page as my introductory example of being impaired. I quickly changed my mind when I opened to 2 Samuel 4:4. I actually like the story of Mephibosheth and it is an excellent example of someone who is impaired, but I decided to just keep it simple and start at the beginning in Genesis with Adam (much easier to type and spell, not to mention how my pronunciation of Mephibosheth would sound on an audio book).

In Genesis 3 we read of the 'fall of man' which some might argue was all Eve's fault. I have searched the bible for a reference that puts the fall of man on the action taken by Eve, but it is not there. Even though Adam was quick to blame Eve, and similarly blame God for creating her, the fall of man sits squarely on the impaired man, Adam. Verse six of chapter three exposes the truth for what it is.

6 *When the woman saw that the fruit of the tree was good for food and pleasing to the eye, and also desirable for gaining wisdom, she took some and ate it. She also gave some to her husband, who was with her, and he ate it.* 7 *Then the eyes of both of them were opened, and they realized they were naked; so they sewed fig leaves together and made coverings for themselves.*

"She also gave some to her husband, who was with her, and he ate it" is the key to our impairment. Adam was with her. He stood there watching, listening, and allowing this scene to play out between the serpent and his wife. What was he thinking? How could he just stand there and not intervene? Why did he not protect his wife? Perhaps he had become so comfortable in the degree of God's love that he lost sight of the decree of God's rule. (I expound on the 'rule' in the chapter, Himmutable.)

There is no difference between myself and Adam. How often do I slip into the lie? I stand by and watch the lie, listen to the lie, participate in the lie, and quickly look to blame someone, something, or even God, for my actions, and then the consequences. Adam was impaired by his imperfect self. I am impaired by my imperfect self. You are impaired by your imperfect self.

Yet God so loved the world He gave his one and only Son, that the impaired who believes in him shall not perish but have eternal life.

Through Jesus Christ, the impaired are Himpaired. The imperfect are made Himperfect. The weakened are strengthened.

Let's take a look at the 19th Chapter of Luke where we read about Zacchaeus.

Jesus entered Jericho and was passing through. [2] A man was there by the name of Zacchaeus; he was a chief tax collector and was wealthy.[3] He wanted to see who Jesus was, but because he was short, he could not see over the crowd. [4] So he ran ahead and climbed a sycamore-fig tree to see him, since Jesus was coming that way. [5] When Jesus reached the spot, he looked up and said to him, "Zacchaeus, come down immediately. I must stay at your house today."[6] So he came down at once and welcomed him gladly. [7] All the people saw this and began to mutter, "He has gone to be the guest of a sinner."
[8] But Zacchaeus stood up and said to the Lord, "Look, Lord! Here and now, I give half of my possessions to the poor, and if I have cheated anybody out of anything, I will pay back four times the amount."
[9] Jesus said to him, "Today salvation has come to this house, because this man, too, is a son of Abraham. [10] For the Son of Man came to seek and to save the lost."

Zacchaeus was obviously impaired by his physical height, but do not overlook his other impairments. Zacchaeus was also impaired by his wealth, his occupation as a tax collector, and according to "all the people", he was also a sinner. So, Zacchaeus was a short, wealthy, tax-collecting sinner.

But Zacchaeus ran ahead and climbed a tree; he was desperate for Jesus. Zacchaeus stood up and said to Jesus, "Look Lord! Here and now..." In his desperation Zacchaeus pursued Jesus.

The Book of Luke also shares a story of a woman who has been bleeding for several years.

40 On the other side of the lake the crowds welcomed Jesus, because they had been waiting for him. 41 Then a man named Jairus, a leader of the local synagogue, came and fell at Jesus' feet, pleading with him to come home with him. 42 His only daughter,[f] who was about twelve years old, was dying.
As Jesus went with him, he was surrounded by the crowds. 43 A woman in the crowd had suffered for twelve years with constant bleeding,[g] and she could find no cure. 44 Coming up behind Jesus, she touched the fringe of his robe. Immediately, the bleeding stopped. 45 "Who touched me?" Jesus asked.
Everyone denied it, and Peter said, "Master, this whole crowd is pressing up against you."
46 But Jesus said, "Someone deliberately touched me, for I felt healing power go out from me." 47 When the woman realized that she could not stay hidden, she began to tremble and fell to her knees in front of him. The whole crowd heard her explain why she had touched him and that she had been immediately healed. 48 "Daughter," he said to her, "your faith has made you well. Go in peace."

The woman was impaired by years of an incurable physical illness and the inconvenience of Jesus being surrounded by a large crowd.

But the woman was desperate to be healed so she reached out and simply touched the fringe of Jesus' robe. In her desperation the bleeding woman pursued Jesus.

One of my favorite stories comes from the second chapter of Mark.

When Jesus returned to Capernaum several days later, the news spread quickly that he was back home. [2] Soon the house where he was staying was so packed with visitors that there was no more room, even outside the door. While he was preaching God's word to them, [3] four men arrived carrying a paralyzed man on a mat. [4] They couldn't bring him to Jesus because of the crowd, so they dug a hole through the roof above his head. Then they lowered the man on his mat, right down in front of Jesus. [5] Seeing their faith, Jesus said to the paralyzed man, "My child, your sins are forgiven." [6] But some of the teachers of religious law who were sitting there thought to themselves, [7] "What is he saying? This is blasphemy! Only God can forgive sins!"
[8] Jesus knew immediately what they were thinking, so he asked them, "Why do you question this in your hearts? [9] Is it easier to say to the paralyzed man 'Your sins are forgiven,' or 'Stand up, pick up your mat, and walk'? [10] So I will prove to you that the Son of Man has the authority on earth to forgive sins." Then Jesus turned to the paralyzed man and said, [11] "Stand up, pick up your mat, and go home!"
[12] And the man jumped up, grabbed his mat, and walked out through the stunned onlookers. They were all amazed and praised God, exclaiming, "We've never seen anything like this before!"

The man was impaired by paralysis; the four men were impaired by logistics. But, four men, desperate to take the paralyzed man to Jesus, dug a hole in the roof and lowered the paralytic down to the floor, directly at the feet of Jesus.

Let's stay in that story for a minute and consider another element of impairment. Verse six describes what the teachers of religious law were thinking. So, sitting in the VIP section, courtside seats to a miracle, the religious teachers were thinking, 'this is blasphemy'. Jesus knew what they were thinking, so He challenged them with what probably sounded like a trick question. *Is it easier to say to the paralyzed man 'Your sins are forgiven,' or 'Stand up, pick up your mat, and walk'?* Jesus didn't ask them which scenario was possible. He asked them which scenario was easier. Jesus could have simply told the paralyzed man that his sins were forgiven, but Jesus knew then what He knows now, there are times when we need to see to believe. The paralyzed man jumped up, picked up his mat, and walked out through the crowd.

They witnessed a miracle, yet their religion impaired their ability to recognize it. Even though they saw a paralytic healed, their religiosity caused them to challenge the truth of Jesus.

The church has become filled with attitudes infected with religious beliefs that create division. Might I suggest the distinct possibility there are times when religion impairs our faith? Might I also suggest religion impairs the Church?

Can you imagine what would happen if Jesus visited Dallas next Sunday morning? Walking down the street he asks some friendly folks where the church is. Which one, they answer. We probably laugh at that answer, but I do not think Jesus would laugh. In Matthew 16, Jesus proclaimed, *"Now I say to you that you are Peter (which means 'rock'), and upon this rock I will build my church."* Jesus did not proclaim He would build a variety of denominations.

The church has become impaired by religiosity and division. Church programs, denominational doctrines, red carpet vs. blue carpet, chairs vs. pews, sprinkling vs. dunking, bread vs. wafer, wine vs. juice, Saturday vs. Sunday, traditional hymns vs. contemporary worship, drive to church vs. watch from couch, etc....

The doctrine of opinion, fueled by our ability to twist His truth to fit personal and societal agendas, has created a plethora of buildings with sparsely filled pews/chairs.

The story of Lazarus from the eleventh chapter of the Book of John is another favorite story. As you read the story below, consider the different aspects of impairment. I have invoked my writer's privilege and embedded (in bold) a few 'impairments' revealed in this story.

A man named Lazarus was sick. He lived in Bethany with his sisters, Mary and Martha. 2 This is the Mary who later poured the expensive perfume on the Lord's feet and wiped them with her hair. Her brother, Lazarus, was sick. **(Impaired by illness)** 3 so the two sisters sent a message to Jesus telling him, "Lord, your dear friend is very sick." 4 But when Jesus heard about it he said, "Lazarus's sickness will not end in death. No, it happened for the glory of God so that the Son of God will receive glory from this." 5 So although Jesus loved Martha, Mary, and Lazarus, 6 he stayed where he was for the next two days. 7 Finally, he said to his disciples, "Let's go back to Judea." 8 But his disciples objected. "Rabbi," they said, "only a few days ago the people in Judea were trying to stone you. **(Impaired by fear)** Are you going there again?" 9 Jesus replied, "There are twelve hours of daylight every day. During the day people can walk safely. They can see because they have the light of this world. 10 But at night there is danger of stumbling because they have no light." 11 Then he said, "Our friend Lazarus has fallen asleep, but now I will go and wake him up." 12 The disciples said, "Lord, if he is sleeping, he will soon get better!" **(Impaired by confusion)** 13 they thought Jesus meant Lazarus was simply sleeping, but Jesus meant Lazarus had died. 14 So he told them plainly, "Lazarus is dead. 15 And for your sakes, I'm glad I wasn't there, for now you will really believe. Come, let's go see him." 16 Thomas, nicknamed the Twin, said to his fellow disciples, "Let's go, too—and die with Jesus." **(Impaired by zeal)** When Jesus arrived at Bethany, he was told that Lazarus had already been in his grave for four days. 18 Bethany was only a few miles down the road from Jerusalem, 19 and many of the people had come to console Martha and Mary in their loss. 20 When Martha got word that Jesus was coming, she went to meet him. But Mary stayed in the house. 21 Martha said to Jesus, "Lord, if only you had been here, my brother would not have died. 22 But even now I know that

God will give you whatever you ask." 23 Jesus told her, "Your brother
will rise again." 24 "Yes," Martha said, "he will rise when everyone
else rises, at the last day."
25 Jesus told her, "I am the resurrection and the life. Anyone who
believes in me will live, even after dying. 26 Everyone who lives in me
and believes in me will never ever die. Do you believe this, Martha?"
27 "Yes, Lord," she told him. "I have always believed you are the
Messiah, the Son of God, the one who has come into the world from
God." 28 Then she returned to Mary. She called Mary aside from the
mourners and told her, "The Teacher is here and wants to see
you." 29 So Mary immediately went to him.
30 Jesus had stayed outside the village, at the place where Martha
met him. 31 When the people who were at the house consoling Mary
saw her leave so hastily, they assumed she was going to Lazarus's
grave to weep. So they followed her there. 32 When Mary arrived and
saw Jesus, she fell at his feet and said, "Lord, if only you had been
here, my brother would not have died."**(Impaired by grief and
sorrow)** 33 When Jesus saw her weeping and saw the other people
wailing with her, a deep anger welled up within him, and he was
deeply troubled.34 "Where have you put him?" he asked them. They
told him, "Lord, come and see." 35 Then Jesus wept. 36 The people
who were standing nearby said, "See how much he loved
him!" 37 But some said, "This man healed a blind man. Couldn't he
have kept Lazarus from dying?"**(Impaired by confusion)** 38 Jesus was
still angry as he arrived at the tomb, a cave with a stone rolled
across its entrance. **(Impaired by a big stone)** 39 "Roll the stone
aside," Jesus told them.
But Martha, the dead man's sister, protested, "Lord, he has been
dead for four days. The smell will be terrible."**(Impaired by logic)**
40 Jesus responded, "Didn't I tell you that you would see God's glory
if you believe?" 41 So they rolled the stone aside. Then Jesus looked
up to heaven and said, "Father, thank you for hearing me. 42 You
always hear me, but I said it out loud for the sake of all these people
standing here, so that they will believe you sent me." 43 Then Jesus
shouted, "Lazarus, come out!" 44 And the dead man came out, his
hands and feet bound in grave clothes, his face wrapped in a head

cloth. **(Impaired by being bound)** Jesus told them, "Unwrap him and let him go!"

You may have identified other impairments, but let's just consider the ones I identified in the bold text; illness, fear, confusion, zeal, grief, sorrow, logic, a big rock, and bondage. The truth is we can relate to being impaired by our own illness or the illness of someone close to us. Being impaired by fear creeps into our lives in many ways. Confusion impairs our ability to cope. For me, zeal is a significant impairment as there are moments when my zeal for something to happen, can push me out of alignment with God's plan for my life. Zeal, fueled by a portion of self-proclaimed rightness, is only problematic when I am forced to attempt to dig my way out of an unfiltered comment or hasty decision. Being impaired by grief and sorrow causes us to either withdraw or become angry. The emotions are real, necessary and expected, but unchecked both sorrow and grief can cause us to be physically, emotionally, relationally, and psychologically impaired. And then there's logic. Logic impairs our ability to accept and understand the super natural, unbelievable ways of our Creator. Isaiah 55:8 says,
"My thoughts are nothing like your thoughts," says the LORD.
"And my ways are far beyond anything you could imagine. The world, in its unquenched desire for control and power depends on logic. We tend to manipulate our logic to justify our opinion which seldom reflects God's truth.

Life needs to be logical, line up in nice rows, and explainable. Logic seeks to remove a Creator. Logic seeks to remove the cross. Logic has no need of an empty tomb. Logic claims to provide an answer. It may be totally wrong, but at least we have an answer. Logic forbids the miracle. Logic activates the lie because it is not plausible for a dead man to walk out of a tomb.

Finally, let's consider being impaired by a big rock. Two different 'big rock' scenarios are worth discussing. The first one is provided above in the Lazarus story; the cave where the body of Lazarus had been placed four days earlier had been sealed with a large stone. Behind the stone was death, darkness, bondage, and hopelessness.

"Roll the stone aside," Jesus told them. In order for Lazarus to walk out of the tomb the big rock had to roll. There was an obstacle and there always is. This scenario is amazing to me. Jesus knew exactly how this was going to play out. He knew there would be people gathered. Normal people. Logical people. Some perhaps were following Him, some were there to comfort Mary and Martha, and some may have just been passing by. And now some of them were about to participate in His purpose. So, just as Jesus had instructed, they moved the big rock. Now what?

I love this. The illogical purpose for Jesus delaying four days to answer Mary's and Martha's request was about to unfold. Jesus looked up to heaven and said, "Father, thank you for hearing me. You always hear me, but I said it out loud for the sake of all these people standing here, so that they will believe you sent me." Jesus had apparently already made his request to God the Father, but Jesus made the request out loud for everyone to hear. Then Jesus shouted, "Lazarus, come out!"

And the dead man came out, his hands and feet bound in grave clothes, with his face wrapped in a head cloth. What? That's illogical. That's impossible. Correct. That was a miracle.

Lazarus was impaired by being dead.

But Jesus spoke his name. When Jesus calls your name, go. The big rock obstacles will be moved. The junk that binds you will be removed, perhaps by someone who just seems to be hanging around. What's so amazing is that Jesus doesn't just call the impaired, He also calls those in proximity to participate 'illogically' in something that no one understands.

Are you finding yourself in these stories of being impaired? I do not have a lot in common with Zacchaeus except for the sinner part. I am thankful that I have nothing in common with the bleeding woman. I can recall those moments in my life when I have been, in a sense, paralyzed. I am thankful for the people in my life who refused to let me sit on my mat of self-pity-paralysis as they carried me back to Jesus.

It is amazing to see the different characteristics of the Lazarus story as they correlate with my life. I have been impaired by His timing. I have been impaired by my anger and His lack of a satisfactory resolution. For five years, 2012-2017, my faith most resembled an unpredictable roller coaster. Sometimes we find ourselves in the front seat of a ride that we really don't want to be on. Strapped in for what I prayed was a very short ride, the uphill climb began. So, for five years I sat, trapped in this extremely binding seat hanging on to the hope in a faith that assured me God was with, and protecting, Melissa. As she persevered through a tough relationship, I was impaired by darkness created by a big rock of fear. I was impaired, stumbling through life, spinning around in a dark place, blinded by the lies of the enemy and a fractured faith. I could not see anything except an unexplainable path of confusion.

What I could see was my precious daughter becoming depressed, drifting away into an unhealthy relationship. Daddy fixes things, but I could not fix this. My fear of accelerating her separation from our family caused me to remain silent. I was sitting on this ride, watching, crying, praying and waiting. My relentless discussion with Jesus went like this; "Jesus, what are you doing sir? (I always tried to stay respectful) What are you waiting for?" I completely understand the anguish of Mary and Martha. And then, March 19, 2017, Melissa walked in our front door. She had been called out of a darkness that I did not fully understand. I still don't understand. I hope and pray I never forget the joy I felt as she walked in the front door of our home, the same home she lived in from first grade through high school. The same home that provided her comfort, safety, and unconditional love. All I could think was, "welcome home" baby girl. The child has a hunger needing to be fed, a longing to be loved, and a desire to be clean.

Because of the miracle unfolding since Melissa's homecoming, I have resolved there was purpose in the delay. Jesus explained to the disciples they would need to wait a few days before going to where Lazarus was buried. There was purpose in the delay. Jesus told them, "This happened for the glory of God so that the Son of God will receive glory from this, and for your sakes, I'm glad I wasn't there, for now you will really believe."
Trust me, our family fully embraces the idea that our journey happened for the glory of God so the Son of God will receive the glory.

When Lazarus walked out of the darkness, stepping into the light of freedom, everyone knew it was a miracle. And they really believed.

When Melissa walked out of her darkness, stepping into the light of freedom (and our home), everyone knew it was a miracle. Thank you, Jesus! We really believe.

I wish I could find the appropriate words to somehow paint a picture of our Lazarus moment. I suspect my problem is similar to someone trying to explain what they saw happen with Lazarus. I have replayed that Sunday morning many times. Melissa called around 8:00 AM to ask if it was OK if she dropped by. I knew she was on her way. Just like December 28, 1985, I knew she was on her way. She had been on her way for nine months. I will never forget the moment (and neither will Pati because her epidural only worked on one side). As Melissa made her way into our hearts and home, I promised to love and protect her. As I took her into my arms, I knew I had to protect her. She was precious. And then, 32 years later, as she made her way back into our home on that Sunday morning, I took her into my arms and thanked God for protecting her. She is precious. From impaired to Himpaired to repaired.

But wait, I have more. In December of 2017, after almost 18 years, my employer told me, and I quote, "you are no longer essential". Being no longer essential meant I would no longer have a job, effective February 5, 2018. Let me list the ways in which this communication impaired me. This impaired my financial plans that included a new Ford F150, my retirement plans, my vacation plans, my image, my marriage, my relationships, my sleep pattern, my eating habits, my my my!

A fascinating reality emerged as I was called into an emergency Starbucks meeting with my dear friend Chris. I had asked him to read the initial draft of this book and after only two days he sent me a text message stating the need for the emergency meeting. One of his observations was an element of impairment related to my career. During my eighteen-year run at AT&T it seems that I had expressed to Chris more than once that I was not overly enthused with my career. It is quite possible embracing a career can impair our yearning to pursue Him, and His call upon our life. It is an unequivocal reality - comfort is a great distractor for me. Thank you, AT&T, for cutting me loose and giving me back my time, my marriage, my relationships, my vacation time, etc... And it seems AT&T was actually correct in declaring me as 'non-essential'. The company has done just fine without me.

It was in my moment of impaired identity that I reached a point of desperation and pursued Jesus. Just like Zacchaeus, I said, "Look Lord! Here and now..." Just like the ill woman I pushed through the crowd and noise to be close to Him. And just like the paralyzed man I had Godly men in my life who refused to leave me outside and made certain I was in His presence.

Impaired? Yes, I am. Fear, shame, guilt, pride, and doubt. Himpaired? Yes, I am. Grace, mercy and unconditional love will do that. Thank You Lord Jesus!

The list of impaired moments and impaired biblical characters goes on and on, page after page, and reflecting a wide array of impairments. And with every birth we welcome into the world the next impaired 'self' whom God loves so much, he sent his Son so that the impaired precious child might one day be desperate for

Jesus, to be Himpaired. What impairs you? What is keeping you from the life God desires for you? Truth is, whether or not you choose to say it, God already knows. He just wants you to be Himpaired. Give your impaired life to Him. Receive His redemption and walk in the light, unbound by stuff. Wherever you are and whatever you may be going through, I pray that you will pray to be desperate for Jesus. Be Himpaired.

Him Still Changes Everything

Chapter 1 Himpaired

Reflections

Are you impaired? There is no need to spend a lot of time trying to discern a profound response to that question. The answer is yes. But you may be asking the other question now; impaired from what? That's a fair question so take some time to reflect on these. As you meditate on each one, ask the Holy Spirit to reveal the need for Him to influence each one. How might you invite Him into each of these areas of your life?

1. Your faith journey
2. Your family
3. Your job / career
4. Your friends
5. Your church
6. Your thoughts
7. Your past
8. Your present

Regarding each of those noted above, which one seems to be the most impaired?

What seems to be the most significant obstacle of your daily walk that impairs you from pursuing your full identity in Jesus Christ?

1. Time
2. Finances
3. Family Relationships
4. Friend Relationships
5. Work / Career
6. Religion
7. Technology (TV, Social Media, Internet)
8. Hobbies
9. Past choices
10. Health
11. List others as you need

Knowing Jesus is calling your name, pray right now for Him to remove the rock(s) listed above so you can confidently walk toward His voice.

Identify the participants in your life who are going to pick you up and remove your bindings. Write their names below and tell them.

Whose life are you participating in and will pick up their mat and remove their bindings. Write their names and tell them.

You are Himpaired - an imperfect or weakened state or condition overcome by faith in Jesus Christ.

Your relationship with Him.... Changes Everything

Chapter 2 Himerica

I love my country. As I look back on my life, there is one glaring regret for me and that is the missed opportunity I had to serve in the military. I live out the blessed life of the freedom bestowed upon me as a citizen of the United States of America. 'Thank you' is woefully insufficient as an expression of gratitude for those who did serve, are serving, and will serve in the Armed Forces of the United States of America. I pray fervently that my children, grandchildren, and all future generations will remember and honor the men and women who sacrificially serve so that we may continue to live in a country embracing the fundamental liberties realized in 'One Nation under God, indivisible, with liberty and justice for all'.

I Pledge Allegiance to the flag
of the United States of America
and to the Republic
for which it stands,
one Nation under God,
indivisible,
with liberty and justice for all.

What was once a declaration of our identity, **One Nation under God, indivisible, with liberty and justice for all**, has become a distant, almost forgotten, opinion. I am writing this chapter during an unprecedented season of chaos in our country and world. I say unprecedented but the reality is history does repeat itself so welcome back Sodom and Gomorrah. The enemy of our day looks and smells just like the enemy in the Garden of Eden. The enemy that introduced sin in the Garden is relentless today in his efforts to deceive, destroy and kill, and has infected every pillar of our society, impacting every thread of our country.

We are quite familiar with the first verse of our National anthem.

O say can you see, by the dawn's early light,
What so proudly we hailed at the twilight's last gleaming,
Whose broad stripes and bright stars through the perilous fight,
O'er the ramparts we watched, were so gallantly streaming.
And the rockets' red glare, the bombs bursting in air,
Gave proof through the night that our flag was still there;
O say does that star-spangled banner yet wave
O'er the land of the free and the home of the brave.

I do not remember the first time I was aware that the Star Spangled Banner had multiple verses, but let's take a look at the fourth verse of our National anthem.

O thus be it ever, when freemen shall stand
Between their loved homes and the war's desolation.
Blest with victory and peace, may the Heaven-rescued land
Praise the Power that hath made and preserved us a nation!
Then conquer we must, when our cause it is just,
And this be our motto: 'In God is our trust.'
And the star-spangled banner in triumph shall wave
O'er the land of the free and the home of the brave!

Repeat: Blessed with victory and peace, may this Heaven-rescued land praise the Power that has made and preserved our nation. Therefore, we must conquer when our cause is just. And this is our motto: 'In God we trust'.

When was the last time a news anchor, politician, famous athlete or entertainer, actually praise the Power that has made and preserved our nation? When is the last time you and I, boldly praised the Power? In our present state of chaos, fueled by an unending relentless barrage of self-serving opinion launched too easily onto the waves of media outlets and social media, we do not know who

to believe. The professional pontificators of opinion have embraced the playground-bully mentality that whoever can yell the loudest for the longest wins. The actual truth has become irrelevant.
We need to get the word out to those who have the platform, we want to know the actual truth. I have no interest in what the 'news' outlets share as what they believe should be truth or what they wish was the truth. And while we are at it, can we also let them know that increasing the volume by which they share their opinion does NOT increase its validity.

The freedom of speech upon which we place great value has been diluted to the point it seems to be okay to say whatever we want without regard for consequences. I remember quite well as a young boy expressing my freedom of speech to my parents. I remember quite well as a young boy the consequences of abusing that freedom. The freedom of speech was not taken away from me but I gained a great respect and understanding of the great responsibility bound by the freedom. And let us not discount the significant consequences when I lied.

What will it take for our country to Himbrace (chapter 7, Him Changes Everything) the truths that formed the foundation of our United States of America?

This topic, Himerica, is worthy of its own book. The greatness of the United States of America can be illustrated in numerous contexts. Even in our imperfections there is an understated pride to be a citizen of the United States of America. It is actually a privilege taken for granted. Yes, I take this privilege for granted. It is worth fighting for and we should fight FOR the privilege. There is a moment in time that it could all change. Unless we decide to seek the God blessed identity that our founders created, the privilege will be history.

If I decide to author the book, Himerica, here are some thoughts regrading chapter titles.

1. The United States of America with God – What was it like
2. The United States of America without God – What is it like

There is a good chance the book, Himerica, or even this book, will not be widely read by a secular audience so I do not need to expand.

Prayer:
Almighty God, creator of all, we plead Your grace and mercy will sustain us and strengthen us to repent of our politically correct tolerance of ourselves and to turn our eyes, minds, and hearts to Your truth, forgiveness and unfailing love. Forgive us of our self-serving agendas and hateful perceptions of those whom we do not take the time to know. Lord, we beg You to soften our hearts for goodness and give us a tenacious Spirit to act upon Your promises, Your truth, and Your goodness with the boldness secured by the belt of truth and the body armor of Your righteousness, the peace of the fulfillment of Your Good News, protected by the shield of faith, covered by Your promise of salvation, and armed with Your Word. Lord, guide us with a united, single-minded focus to once again be One Nation, under God, indivisible, with liberty and justice for all. Amen.

Chapter 2 Himerica

Reflections

1. Please pray for the leaders of our country.
2. Please pray for the leaders of our states.
3. Please pray for the leaders of our counties.
4. Please pray for the leaders of our cities.
5. Please pray for the leaders of our schools.
6. Please pray for the leaders of our churches.
7. Please pray for the leaders of our families.

Do you have a specific person or issue that you will dedicate to prayer?

What do you believe to be the most significant issues with each of the statements 1-7?

Your faith in Him.... Changes Everything

Chapter 3 Himmutable

Immutable

Unable to be changed

Himmutable

God is unchanged

"As long as you live under this roof you will do what I say and live by my rules!" I wonder how many times I heard that declared during my childhood. I was reminded of the rules every day. The repetition was not due to mom's forgetfulness. The repetition was required because I was a rather cantankerous red-headed child. I knew the rules. I simply found it necessary to challenge the rules. For example, I was keenly aware of the rule that I was not to play with sharp objects. Even as a six-year-old little kid I understood that rule. Sharp objects tend to hurt little red-headed kids. I understood the rule. So one has to wonder, how in the world did this happen.

I was playing a lively game of front-yard football with my best friend and his older brother. The older, wiser brother was at least nine years old. We were playing football in their front yard which was almost directly across the street from my house on 66th Street in Lubbock, TX. The football rolled into the bushy hedges and as I was retrieving it through the dirt and dead leaves... SCORE! JACKPOT! ... I found an old dirty, rusted icepick. A treasure for an adventurous couple of little kids, so the new adventure began. The older, wiser brother decided that playing hand grenades was a perfect game for an old rusted icepick and two six-year-olds. We had played this game many times, but we normally used a harmless dirt clod as the hand grenade. The object of the game was for the 'grenade launcher' to ride his bicycle from driveway to driveway, and while peddling with all his might, riding at max speed, to throw a dirt clod in the direction of the 'enemy'. Whoever was closest to the dirt clod as it came to a complete stop, was 'blown up'.

An invigorating activity on its own merit, but when you replace the harmless dirt clod with an old rusted icepick the sheer excitement of this harmless game reached unimaginable levels of exhilaration.

Let the games begin. The older wiser brother decided he would be the grenade launcher which left me and my best friend to act out the role of the 'enemy'. So, there we stood, like six-year-old SEAL Team Six soldiers, in the middle of the battlefield, preparing for one of us to be blown up. As the grenade launcher mounted his 3-speed Stingray with a banana seat and peddled madly to reach max speed, the 'hand grenade' (ice pick) was launched. Within a second, I was blown up; the icepick came to a complete stop as it entered my chest. I fell backward, flat on my back, as both of my friends began to scream. My sister was almost hit by a car as she ran across the street without stopping and looking both ways (another broken rule). There was an icepick stuck in my chest, but I was barely bleeding. Full-fledged panic was upon us. The screaming increased and finally got the attention of my friends' mom. I was laying on my back in her front yard with an icepick protruding from my chest.

I don't remember who it was, but somebody removed it and nothing happened. The icepick had stuck in a rib. My mom dressed the wound and called our doctor. She explained what happened and that was it. I know, fairly anti-climactic. But what if? What if the icepick had been a quarter inch in any direction? A punctured lung or heart. Potentially fatal.

I knew the 'sharp objects' rule. Do not play with sharp objects. And as a parent and now grandparent, that rule has not changed and will never change… it is immutable … unchanging. We get confused when the rules change, but that rule had not changed, I was not confused, I simply chose to disobey.

In the second chapter of Genesis, God created man, placed him in the garden, and told him the rule (there was only one). Do not eat the fruit from that tree. That one right there. See it? That one... do NOT eat from that one. You can eat from every other tree in this garden paradise; all of them. However, that tree, yes that one tree, is the only one you cannot eat from. I have a vision of God expanding His arms out and showing Adam the vastness of Godly provision in the Garden. And then, pointing again to that one tree, confirming that Adam knew exactly which tree was off limits. Then God created woman and placed her in the garden with Adam. In the third chapter, we see where Eve is repeating the rule to the serpent. It is clear Adam and Eve knew the rule and had enjoyed their life in the garden in the presence of the Creator. They had everything they could possibly ever need. Who knows how many times they had passed by the forbidden tree without any regard for partaking of its fruit. They knew the rule.

The beauty, peace, tranquility, innocence, purity, and life in that garden is beyond my imagination. And then, Satan appeared and introduced deception and confusion. He does not change the garden; he introduces sin into the garden. Eve repeated the rule to Satan. The one rule had not changed, yet it was now being challenged. It was being challenged with a lie to somehow feed the self-serving curious nature and subsequent desire...we call it temptation. And with Adam standing by watching the scene unfold, Eve took a piece of fruit from that forbidden tree, ate some and then shared it with Adam. Yes, Adam was standing right there with her.

Amid the vast provision was one simple rule. God told them not to eat of one tree, but to enjoy His unlimited provision of everything they could ever need.

Several years ago I was teaching sixth grade Sunday School and had created some curriculum called Sunday's Cool. When you say it out loud it sounds like Sunday School. (you really did just say it out loud didn't you). I made up some very strange words to teach different lessons and the word for this lesson was derived from the phrase, 'come on, it was just a piece of fruit... comniwajapof (COMe oN It WAs Just A Piece Of Fruit) To illustrate the lesson I put a bowl of candy on a chair and told the kids not to eat any until I returned. One rule. My accomplice was the quietest girl in the class. She was the most respectful, most shy, most obedient kid in the class. I talked to her mom and dad, explaining the lesson, and they were 'all in'.

Shortly after I left the classroom my accomplice walked in and ever so innocently took a seat. My accomplice then walked over to the candy bowl and took a piece. The good news was the other kids told her she could not have any until I returned. She said to the class, "Do you really think Mr. Gann would sit candy in a chair where we can reach it if he really didn't want us to eat it? I am sure he would have put it out of our reach if he didn't want us to eat it." Apparently, deep logic coming from my cute little accomplice was all that was needed to get the majority of the class to partake of the forbidden candy.

The class understood the rule, they shared the rule, and they disobeyed the rule. The consequence was chaos. When I returned, before the door even closed behind me, the kids who had obeyed were very quick to share the names of those who broke the rule. And then, without any prompting, one of the guilty boys said these exact words, "it was her fault", pointing to my cute little accomplice.

Just like the scene in the Garden, Adam said, "it was her fault." The very same logic I used when the local law enforcement officer asked me why I was speeding; it was Pati's fault. I knew the speed limit (the rule). It had been the same speed limit for over twenty years. The rule had not been changed to trick me. I knew the rule.

I don't know about you, but I have a 'love-hate' relationship with rules. I love rules when they provide peace for my life, but I hate those very same rules when they create distress in my life.

The good news for us is that God has not changed. His truth is Himmutable. **His truth imparts order when His creation aligns with His purpose.** In Matthew, chapter 22: verses 36-40, Jesus was asked which commandment was the most important. He stated, "love the Lord your God with all your heart, soul and mind. This is the first and greatest commandment. A second is equally important. Love your neighbor as yourself." Paraphrasing what Jesus said, the most important rule is for me to love God and others more than I love myself. I have not been made aware that God has changed the rule.

Hebrews 13:8 reminds us that Jesus Christ is the same yesterday, today, and forever.

I wrote this chapter during the 2020 presidential campaign between Donald Trump and Joe Biden; oops, Kamala Harris. . At some point during the campaign, each candidate expressed their faith belief. Donald Trump professed to be a 'non-denominational' Christian. Kamala Harris professes to be a Baptist and Joe professed as a Catholic. Some of you may be surprised by this, but a ***few*** politicians will say whatever they think their audience wants to hear. Based on what I heard from them on every news outlet, Donald, Joe, and Kamala, lost sight of God's most important rule. As they raced furiously from driveway to driveway, peddling their opposition's imperfections, they launched unfiltered hate grenades which came to a complete stop in the chest of the United States of America. And yes, chaos ran rampant. From the mouths of many who hold powerful positions come lies and name-calling. These folks deserve nothing less than a swift kick in the butt, a boxing lesson in the garage with my dad, or some belt action from my mom. They have no fear of consequences.

I don't lie (oops) and I don't call people names unless I am driving and they deserve it. Our self-serving opinions do not dictate or define a new truth for everyone else. Opinion does not change truth; it simply adds a narrative blurring the truth. I believe there is one truth. My choice, and your choice, **is to trust His truth in faith or twist the truth to fit.**

The rule has not changed nor is God going to change the rule to fit our self-serving culture. He is not going to redefine 'neighbor' to fit those who are easy to love. My plea is for His creation to love Him most so they can love everyone better. Yes. Everyone!

The Sermon on the Mount teaching from the fifth chapter of Matthew provides uncluttered, clear direction.

43 "You have heard that it was said, 'Love your neighbor[i] and hate your enemy.' 44 But I tell you, love your enemies and pray for those who persecute you, 45 that you may be children of your Father in heaven. He causes his sun to rise on the evil and the good, and sends rain on the righteous and the unrighteous. 46 If you love those who love you, what reward will you get? Are not even the tax collectors doing that? 47 And if you greet only your own people, what are you doing more than others? Do not even pagans do that? 48 Be perfect, therefore, as your heavenly Father is perfect.

Donald, you should love Joe... Kamala . Joe... Kamala, you should love Donald. The rules have not changed.
That was fun to type, until it made me consider that the scripture applies to me and the 'Donalds', 'Joes', and 'Kamalas ' in my life.

Even though I may not like rules, rules give us a foundation of order. I need the simplicity that the rules should provide. I grew up in the house of calm as long as everyone followed the rules. Be home at 6:00 for dinner did not mean 6:05. It did not matter that the big kids were beating me up (they weren't, and yes, I lied about it). When mom or dad told me to stop doing whatever I was doing, I stopped. Continuing to do what I was told to stop doing always ended poorly for me. I do not ever remember my mom saying, "I am going to count to three and you had better stop before I get to three." The only time I remember mom counting to three was when she was spanking me. I guess she wanted me to realize the difference between the three-swat spanking and the five-swat spanking.

Counting beyond five was irrelevant as I couldn't hear over my sobbing. The good news for me is the Gann house rules did not change.

The good news for us is God has not changed the rules, but that does not mean they are always easy to understand or accept. Have you ever really considered the rule Jesus shared with the disciples in John 14:6? Jesus tells the disciples He will be leaving them soon and someday, they will be with Him again. Obviously, a few questions arose with this announcement and Jesus says, *"I am the way, the truth, and the life. No one can come to the Father except through me."* This declaration reinforces John 3:14-21

"…so the Son of Man must be lifted up, 15 *so that everyone who believes in him will have eternal life.* 16 *"For this is how God loved the world: He gave his one and only Son, so that everyone who believes in him will not perish but have eternal life.* 17 *God sent his Son into the world not to judge the world, but to save the world through him.* 18 *"There is no judgment against anyone who believes in him. But anyone who does not believe in him has already been judged for not believing in God's one and only Son.* 19 *And the judgment is based on this fact: God's light came into the world, but people loved the darkness more than the light, for their actions were evil.* 20 *All who do evil hate the light and refuse to go near it for fear their sins will be exposed.* 21 *But those who do what is right come to the light so others can see that they are doing what God wants."*

The rule is lovingly, graciously, mercifully simple, yet so many refuse it. They want to debate the idea of a loving God having more than one way. They want the convenience of twisting the truth to fit whatever belief system they have embraced. Sadly, there are churches teaching a watered-down version of this simple truth; *"No one can come to the Father except through me."* Jesus said it, I believe it. It's simple for believers who have accepted Jesus Christ as their Lord and Savior. It's eternally tragic for those who don't.

In my simplicity, I wrongly assume simplicity works for everyone, but I know it does not. Below are some supporting scriptures that confirm this rule.

John 3:16 *"For this is how God loved the world: He gave[g] his one and only Son, so that everyone who believes in him will not perish but have eternal life.*

Ephesians 2:8-9 *God saved you by his grace when you believed. And you can't take credit for this; it is a gift from God. 9 Salvation is not a reward for the good things we have done, so none of us can boast about it.*

John 3:36 *And anyone who believes in God's Son has eternal life.*

John 6:47 *I tell you the truth, anyone who believes has eternal life.*

Luke 23 *But the other criminal protested, "Don't you fear God even when you have been sentenced to die? 41 We deserve to die for our crimes, but this man hasn't done anything wrong." 42 Then he said, "Jesus, remember me when you come into your Kingdom." 43 And Jesus replied, "I assure you, today you will be with me in paradise."*

The world view is to live as you want and die. The Good News view is to die to self and live. The polarity of opposition is real and it is eternally serious. That is why God has made it easy for us, just like He did for Adam and Eve in the Garden. Just one rule, choose wisely. For you and me, once again God says there's one way, choose Jesus.

God is immutable, His rules are Himmutable.

Chapter 3 Himmutable

Reflections

1. How do you rate your ability to live out the scripture, ' But I tell you, love your enemies and pray for those who persecute you.' ?

2. Who do you consider to be your enemy?

3. How do you rate your ability to live out the scripture 'love the Lord your God with all your heart, soul and mind.'?

4. How do you rate your ability to live out the scripture 'love your neighbor as yourself.'?

Your trust in Him…. Changes Everything

Chapter 4 Himmature

Immature – not fully developed: lacking wisdom, insight, emotional stability

Himmature – intentionally pursuing fully developed identity in Christ, exhibiting wisdom, insight, and emotional stability

I am a little nervous about writing this chapter because the definition of Himmature might give the reader a sense that I believe I have fully developed my identity in Jesus Christ. It would be rather immature of me to portray myself as Himmature. I know for a fact I am a work in progress. I pray I will continue to have a desire to pursue a fully developed identity in Christ, consistently and intentionally moving toward Himmaturity.

I decided I would return to my days of academia, specifically my graduate studies in professional counseling, in order to gain and share Master's level educational insight on maturity, thus being able to define how we measure both maturity and immaturity. The research and subsequent analysis revealed there is not a proven scientific or psychological study proving a consistent measure of maturity. That being said, I recognize different levels of maturity reflected in my personal life journey will be sufficient for this chapter of in-depth intellectual excavation for nuggets of experiential gems. See, that was a very mature sentence, which only reflects my immaturity in attempting to write like a professional. This is going to be fun.

Some of the research did seem to indicate 18 is a nominally recognized age of maturity. However, I can debunk said research rather quickly. As recognition for graduating from high school without getting thrown in jail, our parents rewarded me and a good friend, a trip to the Grand Canyon as a graduation gift. The really good news was his parents offered to let us drive their new Cadillac to the Grand Canyon. His parents apparently measured our maturity level on a different scale than my parents. My parents overtly questioned their generosity and my dad strongly suggested we should just take my '65 Mustang or my friend's '72 station wagon (the avocado green one with woodgrain panels).

The morning of our departure arrived and after a few minutes of 'pre-travel' rules, my dad pulled me and my mature travel buddy aside and threatened to ruin our lives forever if we let anything happen to the new Cadillac. What was he thinking? Why was he concerned? What could possibly go wrong? These two recent high school grads had soared boldly to the next level of maturity. Didn't dad recognize we had received society's acceptable certification of maturity… the high school diploma? My buddy and I were very mature, represented by our vast arsenal of fireworks secretly stashed in our luggage in the new Cadillac. Seriously, what could possibly go wrong?

Somewhere along the 120 mile stretch of extreme nothingness between Amarillo, Texas and Tucumcari, New Mexico, it was time to get tactical. The stash of fireworks would simply provide enough entertainment to keep us awake on this brain-numbing, amazingly straight stretch of asphalt and dirt, adorned with an occasional mesquite tree. Counting and trying to run over tumbleweeds quickly lost its appeal, plus there was always a chance of hitting a large tumbleweed and scratching the paint on the new Cadillac. The next best mode of entertainment was to see if we could light a smoke bomb with the cigarette lighter (all cars had one) and while maintaining the posted speed limit, toss the lit smoke bomb out the window, getting the smoke bomb to land in the road behind us. Other than a slightly burnt finger, we prevailed and finally arrived in Tucumcari, New Mexico where we enjoyed Papa Burgers, tater tots, and a frosty mug of root beer at the A&W Root Beer Stand. It was time to relax and get some rest so we checked into our motel.

I discovered the Little League baseball field behind our motel and by golly, there were games underway. Under the extremely bright lights were kids, parents, coaches, concession stands, tumbleweeds, and two teams enjoying the evening of spirited competition. Along with the snow cones and the smell of popcorn, I could hear the all-familiar chatter of Little League Baseball. Hey batter batter batter swing! This was a sweet surprise as it reminded me of my childhood baseball days. An additional sweet surprise was the discovery there was not a screen on the window and yes, we had bottle rockets in our arsenal. What could possibly go wrong? Our recently acquired maturity went unchecked.

I was certain the flashing lights and pounding knock on our door were about to shatter our dream of reaching Grand Canyon. Two of Tucumcari's finest law enforcement officers scared the bejeebies out of us. I am certain they enjoyed a good laugh as they confiscated 'most' of our fireworks. They didn't check the Cadillac for additional contraband. As we departed Tucumcari very early the next morning, we were extremely thankful for the warning and the fact we had escaped years of hard labor in the New Mexico Justice System.

The remainder of the trip was uneventful except for the untimely discovery that my buddy was allergic to horse hair. The discovery was made halfway through a two-mile horseback ride into the canyon. He was on the horse behind me and I heard him start sneezing and then our little group had to stop as he went from sneezing to wheezing, to barely breathing. He survived and we were four-wheeled back to the parking lot. New maturity lesson! Make sure you are not allergic to horsehair BEFORE you get a mile into the Grand Canyon on a horse.

Our newly acquired maturity was becoming more and more apparent. We enjoyed touring around in our new Cadillac, jamming to Lynyrd Skynyrd, Boston, Eagles, Chicago, Willie Nelson, the Doobie Brothers, and many others. As we sadly approached our final destination of home, which was approximately two miles away, I began collecting fast-food trash from under my seat and discovered one last smoke bomb. (I should have remembered what happened when I discovered an icepick!) We determined we should conclude our maturity-defining, trail-blazing adventure on a high note, declaring victory by launching this last smoke bomb as we entered our neighborhood. Did I mention we were in a new Cadillac? A new Cadillac that had power windows. Power windows that can be controlled by the driver. For some mature reason, my mature friend somehow determined raising my window at the very moment I was trying to toss the now lit smoke bomb out the window, was mature, in a funny sort of way. Ricocheting off my now closed window, the sizzling smoke bomb rolled under my seat in the new Cadillac. A sizzling HOT smoke bomb is impossible to remove from under one's car seat. It also fills a new Cadillac with a lot of smoke, very quickly. Suddenly, I wished the Tucumcari Police had arrested me. Hard-time in the New Mexico prison system was looking good about now, as I remembered my dad telling me he would "ruin my life" if we let anything happen to the new Cadillac.

We made an unplanned side-trip to the store to purchase a variety of cleaning supplies, one of which was Pine-Sol which has a very strong aroma. We spent the next three hours fumigating, cleaning, and washing, the inside and outside of the new Cadillac. As much as I hate the smell of cigarette smoke, I was so very thankful my buddy's parents smoked. I suspect they spent weeks trying to get the Pine-Sol smell out of their new Cadillac.

Obviously, turning 18 and receiving a high school diploma, are NOT appropriate measures of maturity.

Does our inability to define an acceptable universal moment of maturity in life, also pertain to maturity in our faith? When does that happen? We cruise through life and wake up one day, look in the mirror, and declare to the world, "I have arrived, as of this moment I have reached maturity in my faith and my identity in Christ is fully developed!"

If neither age, certifications, nor accomplishments render a person mature, what does?

In the spring of 2016, some good friends planted a pecan tree in their front yard. Upon its planting day, the diameter of the trunk was approximately an inch. However, the root system on that scrawny tree was significant. The purpose of the root system was to absorb and store water and nutrients, anchor the pecan tree in the ground, and to expand in order to compete with the other plants, so the tree will grow into its maturity, fulfilling its purpose to produce pecans. The maturity of that pecan tree will not be realized until it produces pie-worthy pecans.
Perhaps, similar to the pecan tree, the true measure of our faith maturity is in the fruit we produce. Oh, that sounds good but what sort of fruit can we produce to really be considered a plausible measure of our maturity?

Himmaturity, defined as, fully developed identity in Christ, begins with our roots; roots of worship, prayer, fellowship, and study. Authentic worship of Him, sincere communication with Him through prayer, fellowship with believers seeking Him, and commitment to study His truth, Himpowers (Chapter 6, Him Changes Everything) us to initiate the maturing process. The fruit of this process is realized when our perpetual pursuit of our identity in Christ reflects consistency in the kind of fruit described in Galatians and reinforced in Colossians.

Galatians 5:22… *But the Holy Spirit produces this kind of fruit in our lives: love, joy, peace, patience, kindness, goodness, faithfulness, gentleness, and self-control.*

Colossians 1:9-10 *So we have not stopped praying for you since we first heard about you. We ask God to give you complete knowledge of his will and to give you spiritual wisdom and understanding. Then the way you live will always honor and please the Lord, and your lives will produce every kind of good fruit. All the while, you will grow (mature) as you learn to know God better and better.* (I inserted mature)

Much easier for me to define it, than it is for me to consistently live out each and every day. On my best days, I might get 6 out of 9. However, I know my soul's desire is to keep my roots anchored to His truth, His worship, and His whispers so His unfailing love and faithfulness will sustain me in my 'root-to-fruit' journey to Himmaturity; my fruit producing fully developed identity in Christ.

In Luke Chapter 8 we do get some insight to spiritual immaturity. Verse 13 says, *"The seeds that fell among the thorns represent those who hear the message, but all too quickly the message is crowded out by the cares and riches and pleasures of this life. And so they never grow into maturity."*

We live in a world of thorns of distraction (cares, riches, and pleasures) and instant gratification (all too quickly the message is crowded out), suffocating our Spiritual roots which depend on our worship of Him, serving Him, trusting in Him.

In Ephesians 3 we read, [17] *then Christ will make his home in your hearts as you trust in him. Your roots will grow down into God's love and keep you strong.* [18] *And may you have the power to understand, as all God's people should, how wide, how long, how high, and how deep his love is.* [19] *May you experience the love of Christ, though it is too great to understand fully. Then you will be made complete with all the fullness of life and power that comes from God.*

Do you know someone who reflects the definition of Himmature? Someone who reflects their fully developed identity in Christ? I do not know anyone who reflects a fully developed identity in Christ, but I know a lot of people who are terrific examples of people who wake up every day with their sole purpose to fulfill their soul purpose, which is to seek daily, their fully developed identity in Jesus Christ.

Biblically, perhaps Paul reflects a fully developed identity in Christ. His sole purpose in life was radically changed when God stopped him in his tracks, or actually his horse's tracks. On his Christian-persecuting journey to Damascus, Saul (Paul) had an encounter with almighty God. Just in case you are not familiar with the story, or just need a gentle reminder, read the story below from Acts, Chapter 9.

Meanwhile, Saul was still breathing out murderous threats against
the Lord's disciples. He went to the high priest [2] and asked him for
letters to the synagogues in Damascus, so that if he found any there
who belonged to the Way, whether men or women, he might take
them as prisoners to Jerusalem. [3] As he neared Damascus on his
journey, suddenly a light from heaven flashed around him. [4] He fell
to the ground and heard a voice say to him, "Saul, Saul, why do you
persecute me?"
[5] "Who are you, Lord?" Saul asked.
"I am Jesus, whom you are persecuting," he replied. [6] "Now get up
and go into the city, and you will be told what you must do."
[7] The men traveling with Saul stood there speechless; they heard the
sound but did not see anyone. [8] Saul got up from the ground, but
when he opened his eyes he could see nothing. So they led him by
the hand into Damascus. [9] For three days he was blind, and did not
eat or drink anything. [10] In Damascus there was a disciple named
Ananias. The Lord called to him in a vision, "Ananias!" "Yes, Lord,"
he answered.
[11] The Lord told him, "Go to the house of Judas on Straight Street
and ask for a man from Tarsus named Saul, for he is praying. [12] In a
vision he has seen a man named Ananias come and place his hands
on him to restore his sight." [13] "Lord," Ananias answered, "I have
heard many reports about this man and all the harm he has done to
your holy people in Jerusalem. [14] And he has come here with
authority from the chief priests to arrest all who call on your name."
[15] But the Lord said to Ananias, "Go! This man is my chosen
instrument to proclaim my name to the Gentiles and their kings and
to the people of Israel. [16] I will show him how much he must suffer
for my name."

[17] Then Ananias went to the house and entered it. Placing his hands
on Saul, he said, "Brother Saul, the Lord—Jesus, who appeared to
you on the road as you were coming here—has sent me so that you

may see again and be filled with the Holy Spirit." [18] *Immediately, something like scales fell from Saul's eyes, and he could see again. He got up and was baptized,* [19] *and after taking some food, he regained his strength.*

Saul spent several days with the disciples in Damascus. [20] *At once he began to preach in the synagogues that Jesus is the Son of God.* [21] *All those who heard him were astonished and asked, "Isn't he the man who raised havoc in Jerusalem among those who call on this name? And hasn't he come here to take them as prisoners to the chief priests?"*[22] *Yet Saul grew more and more powerful and baffled the Jews living in Damascus by proving that Jesus is the Messiah.*
[23] *After many days had gone by, there was a conspiracy among the Jews to kill him,* [24] *but Saul learned of their plan. Day and night they kept close watch on the city gates in order to kill him.* [25] *But his followers took him by night and lowered him in a basket through an opening in the wall.*

[26] *When he came to Jerusalem, he tried to join the disciples, but they were all afraid of him, not believing that he really was a disciple.* [27] *But Barnabas took him and brought him to the apostles. He told them how Saul on his journey had seen the Lord and that the Lord had spoken to him, and how in Damascus he had preached fearlessly in the name of Jesus.* [28] *So Saul stayed with them and moved about freely in Jerusalem, speaking boldly in the name of the Lord.* [29] *He talked and debated with the Hellenistic Jews but they tried to kill him.* [30] *When the believers learned of this, they took him down to Caesarea and sent him off to Tarsus.*
[31] *Then the church throughout Judea, Galilee and Samaria enjoyed a time of peace and was strengthened. Living in the fear of the Lord and encouraged by the Holy Spirit, it increased in numbers.*

From an encounter getting his undivided attention, to a three-day period of blindness and fasting, to a physical and spiritual awakening, Paul reached Himmaturity. I love verse 20. The radical Himpact did not cause Paul to request a season of personal reflection. Paul knew, that he knew, that he knew, his sole purpose was to be sold out for Jesus Christ...right now! Verse 20 says he began to preach in the synagogues that Jesus is the Son of God. Then in verse 22 we see the maturing process on steroids. Paul grew more and more powerful. His roots were planted firmly in his unfiltered belief because he was changed, so he could live out with purpose, his full identity, producing fruit. And you can too.

At once he began to preach in the synagogues that Jesus is the Son of God. 21 All those who heard him were astonished and asked, "Isn't he the man who raised havoc in Jerusalem among those who call on this name? And hasn't he come here to take them as prisoners to the chief priests?"22 Yet Saul grew more and more powerful and baffled the Jews living in Damascus by proving that Jesus is the Messiah.

I don't know about you but I truly want to be that changed. I want to be the guy whose behavior causes astonishment with the people. I am redeemed and set free, and by Him, with Him, for Him, my life should reflect the Himmaturity of those truths. I am redeemed and free, to produce His fruit of *love, joy, peace, patience, kindness, goodness, faithfulness, gentleness, and self-control.*

Now that you are motivated to be intentional about seeking to become a Spirit filled fruit-producing Himmature individual, what should the world see? Probably nothing until you are squeezed. You will 'look' good. All shined up on display with Spirit filled fruit-producing Himmature individuals. And then a little pressure gets applied and you get squeezed. It can be a relationship getting twisted, a career going awry or away, a bank account at an all-time low, a driver who is consumed by whatever is on his/her phone and drifts into your lane, or you could just be having a lousy day. Pressure is pressure, no matter the source. When you squeeze a lemon you will get lemon juice. When you squeeze a grape, you get grape juice. You can try to disguise it, but it is grape juice. When you get squeezed, no matter how you attempt to disguise it, the level of your Himmaturity will be exposed.

Peter is one of my favorites. Possibly because I can see and hear myself in how he reacts to situations. In the thirteenth chapter of John, Jesus is telling the disciples what is about to take place. Verse 31 picks up the response and the conversation between Peter and Jesus.

As soon as Judas left the room, Jesus said, "The time has come for the Son of Man[h] to enter into his glory, and God will be glorified because of him. 32 And since God receives glory because of the Son,[i] he will give his own glory to the Son, and he will do so at once. 33 Dear children, I will be with you only a little longer. And as I told the Jewish leaders, you will search for me, but you can't come where I am going. 34 So now I am giving you a new commandment: Love each other. Just as I have loved you, you should love each other. 35 Your love for one another will prove to the world that you are my disciples." 36 Simon Peter asked, "Lord, where are you going?" And Jesus replied, "You can't go with me now, but you will follow me later." 37 ***"But why can't I come now, Lord?" he asked. "I'm ready to die for you." 38 Jesus answered, "Die for me? I tell you the truth, Peter—before the rooster crows tomorrow morning, you will deny three times that you even know me.***

Chapter 18 describes the 'squeeze' that Peter must respond to and ultimately, his level of Himmaturity.

15 Simon Peter followed Jesus, as did another of the disciples. That other disciple was acquainted with the high priest, so he was allowed to enter the high priest's courtyard with Jesus. 16 Peter had to stay outside the gate. Then the disciple who knew the high priest spoke to the woman watching at the gate, and she let Peter in. 17 The woman asked Peter, "You're not one of that man's disciples, are you?" "No," he said, "I am not." 18 Because it was cold, the household servants and the guards had made a charcoal fire. They stood around it, warming themselves, and Peter stood with them, warming himself.

[25] Meanwhile, as Simon Peter was standing by the fire warming himself, they asked him again, "You're not one of his disciples, are you?" He denied it, saying, "No, I am not." [26] But one of the household slaves of the high priest, a relative of the man whose ear Peter had cut off, asked, "Didn't I see you out there in the olive grove with Jesus?" [27] Again Peter denied it. And immediately a rooster crowed.

Peter had a life changing encounter with himself. When squeezed by fear, he responded exactly how Jesus had predicted. Part of me believes Peter must have been really mad at that stupid rooster. The stupid rooster revealed Peter's denial to everyone. As for me, it's not a stupid rooster revealing the truth. For me it's my mirror, my mouth, my attitude, my actions.

In order to withstand the pressures encountered during my journey toward Himmaturity it is imperative for me to make certain my roots of worship, prayer, fellowship, and study are secure. If my roots are poisoned, cut-off, or neglected, my ability to withstand the 'squeeze' will be at risk. I know it works because we see the results played out when Jesus has a miraculous encounter with the disciples and confirms his plan for Peter. We should all be encouraged by the redeeming power and unfailing love of Jesus Christ to right our paths toward Himmaturity.

The fruit produced by Peter as his journey proceeded through the Book of Acts is the encouragement I need to continue to trust, God's plan for me is good. Even when I fail Him, deny Him, neglect Him, His unfailing love, grace and mercy draws me back to embrace Him.

Lord, I pray you will place upon my heart, an unquenchable desire to seek Himmaturity, my fully developed identity in Christ, so the fruit... love, joy, peace, patience, kindness, goodness, faithfulness, gentleness, and self-control will be revealed when I am squeezed.

Your walk with Him.... Changes Everything

Chapter 4 Himmaturity

Reflections

1. How do you define maturity?
2. How do you define spiritual maturity?
3. Which of the fruits of the Spirit are revealed when you are 'squeezed'?
4. As you pursue your identity in Christ, are you aware of the things, people, and activities that distract you?

Your belief in Him…. Changes Everything

Chapter 5 Himitate

> Imitate – to follow or endeavor to follow as model or example
>
> Himitate – to follow Christ or endeavor to follow Christ as a model or example; to be Christ-like

I am not a proponent of negative self-talk. I firmly believe the polarity of our words, negative and positive, induces a behavior reflective of the self-talk. I am a positive person, optimistic about my outlook, and encouraging. So here is my positive, optimistic, encouraging self-talk regarding my golf game. I am positive I am wasting my time, optimistic my drive might surpass the ladies tee box, and encouraged to sell my clubs. However, it seems each and every time I attempt to play, I hit at least one shot causing me to reconsider my self-imposed lifetime ban from the sport.

I suspect at some level, he may still be trying to gain my approval, but Bill (son-in-law) has asked me to play golf on numerous occasions. On one such fun-packed (positive self-talk) outing, we were on a par 5 hole which historically means I am going to lose two balls instead of one. True to form, my enormous tee shot skipped across the water and abruptly settled at the bottom of the pond, no more than twenty-five yards from the tee box. A fairly typical shot and result, which would normally end with a simple walk-off from the tee box, but for some reason, I thought it would be a good idea to drown another golf ball. So, I reached into my pocket, revealing a brand new Titleist ProV1, and assuming it would soon be reunited with my earlier shot in the pond, I admired its dimples and gently kissed it goodbye. I used the same tee, from the same spot, the same driver, same pre-swing concentration, and I am confident the same swing. SMACK. The new ProV1 was screaming through the air like a tomahawk missile. And unlike other airborne shots I had hit, it was going straight down the fairway, a very long way down the fairway.

Bill's response was priceless…?*&"%$&^!!! He reached into his bag and pulled out his fancy little yardage finder binocular, looking down the fairway he repeated his earlier response. He then laughed and said I had just hit that golf ball, which looked just like the pond-ball, 297 yards (he actually rounded up to 300). Let me repeat my earlier statement; it seems each and every time I attempt to play golf, I hit at least one shot that causes me to reconsider my lifetime ban from the sport.

I believe it was that one shot prompting Bill to invite me to join him, Rhonda, and Dustin in a scramble tournament at the Iron Horse Country Club. In full transparency, I do have a certain level of confidence at the previously mentioned course simply because there is not one house anywhere near the course. Unfortunately, the Iron Horse Country Club has many beautiful homes with lots of beautiful targets (also known as windows) throughout the course. As we began our round I had a horrible flashback to a Big Stuff Christian youth camp in Florida several years ago, when a few of us decided to play golf. Mostly because David T. won't let me forget it, the sound of breaking glass as a result of one of my screaming errant tee shots, began to replay itself. It was a terrifyingly horrible sound. And as any good Christian youth counselor should do, I unashamedly blamed it on one of our youths. (I have never claimed to be Himmature)

For me, golf is a frustrating game, but because I have lowered my expectations to meet my capability, I typically have fun just being outdoors and getting exercise walking around looking for my golf balls. The reason I find that enjoyable is that I always find more golf balls other golfers have lost, which made me realize that I am not the only lousy golfer.

I have always considered myself to be fairly competitive in most sports, but golf is just demoralizing. However, my competitive nature caused me to start watching, while napping, PGA tournaments on Sunday afternoons so that I could pick up some pointers from the best players. If I could just stay awake long enough to analyze their swing, then I should be able to imitate it and then surely, I could become a better player. After hours of napping and analyzing their swings, it's time for the driving range. I can honestly say I am still horrible. I can't even fake being a decent golfer. Equipping me with good gear, and placing me on a beautiful golf course, with a tee time on a beautiful morning, has the makings of a great day until I am challenged by teeing up the harmless little white dimpled sphere. The beauty of the moment is radically changed as soon as I am required to go into action. The moment of truth in my ability is revealed as soon as I commit myself to the back-swing. My ability to imitate the best golfer is quickly on display for the world to see. Okay, maybe not the world, but at least the brave souls who are with me and the foursome (unaware targets) behind me.

My backswing does not take a lot of time, but let's say it takes me three seconds to move my club from its resting place behind the ball to the top of my swing, back to the point of impact with the ball. In those three seconds, my mind has processed four elements of negative self-talk based on previous experiences. Fear, doubt, shame, and guilt. Just one of those will suffice in creating enough distraction to keep me from executing a good swing, but I battle all four. I fear someone will see me and laugh at my swing; I doubt that I will hit a decent shot; I am guilty of wasting time and money on this activity; and I experience shame as I know I will be embarrassed as soon as I make contact with the ball (if I indeed make contact with the ball). All of those thoughts happen in my backswing, so there is no chance I am going to hit a good shot. No matter how intentional I am at imitating a great golfer, my past experience on the golf course will always enter my mind and another golf ball will soon retire innocently into a pond, backyard, window, or interstate.

This desire to imitate the best is repeated in other areas of my life as well. I remember wanting to imitate my dad's ability to throw a baseball. In my career, there have been many men and women that have been worthy of imitating in order to increase my capabilities to enhance my career options and opportunities. There are men I recognize as pillars of success in the community so I should imitate them in order for me to have a positive impact on my community.

I have been blessed with many imitate-able people in every facet of my life; career, family, neighborhood, church, community, etc..... I actually started to make a list of the individuals I should imitate in order to be the best I can be in all things, however, I discovered the list is very long. Many different names for the many different elements of life. I am a simple man, simple thinker, so I need a short simple list. Who is that one person I should imitate in order to be the best I can be in every aspect of my life?

In Galatians, Chapter 3:27 we read, *'And all who have been united with Christ in baptism have put on Christ, like putting on new clothes.' And then in Ephesians 4:15, 'Instead, we will speak the truth in love, growing in every way more and more like Christ, who is the head of his body, the church.'*

When I live my life intentionally, with an authentic desire to imitate Him, the enemy's distractions of fear, doubt, guilt, and shame are rendered defeated. An authentic desire to Himitate, eliminates negative self-talk. I know this because an authentic Himitator lives a life of unapologetic, bold love for Jesus Christ, which renders the enemy of lies (negative self-talk) defeated.

I believe I am a better husband and daddy because I watched my dad do his best to imitate Christ with all his heart, all his soul, and all his strength. Yes, I want to imitate that. Let's call it Himitation; to follow Christ or endeavor to follow Christ as a model or example; to be Christ-like.

Watching Godly men stand strong for their faith is just a part of my backswing of living a life for Him. Hebrews 13:7 says, *remember your leaders, who spoke the word of God to you. Consider the outcome of their way of life and imitate their faith. Jesus Christ is the same yesterday and today and forever.*

I encourage you to identify those men and women who are doing their best to Himitate and watch how they love sacrificially and humbly serve, for no other reason than to follow Christ or endeavor to follow Christ as a model or example; to be Christ-like.

Yet, at some point, there is the realization even the best of the best is impaired, so we must look to the One who is truly worthy of our Himitation. And it's stated so simply; You must love the LORD your God with all your heart, all your soul, and all your mind.
In Ephesians 5 we read, ***Imitate God, therefore, in everything you do,*** *because you are his dear children. [2] Live a life filled with love, following the example of Christ. He loved us and offered himself as a sacrifice for us, a pleasing aroma to God.*

And in 1 Corinthians, chapter 4, Paul tells the church in Corinth, *even if you had ten thousand guardians in Christ, you do not have many fathers, for in Christ Jesus I became your father through the gospel. [16] Therefore I urge you* **to imitate me.** *[17] For this reason I have sent to you Timothy, my son whom I love, who is faithful in the Lord. He will remind you of my way of life in Christ Jesus, which agrees with what I teach everywhere in every church.*

I believe it was mid-year 2015 when I was informed by a colleague that a young man (D.J.) had accepted a new position with our organization and was relocating with his young family to the Dallas / Ft. Worth area. My colleague told D.J. to find me as soon as he arrived. I met with D.J. soon after he arrived and before I had an opportunity to ask my set of questions and to educate him on the ins-and-outs of Texas living, he directed the conversation to a place I had not expected. He was not concerned with the nuances of Texanese, but he was very interested in how to maintain his relationship with God. He was very interested in how to continue leading his family as God would have him lead.

I was reminded of the fact my relationship with Him must be my number one priority because others may be looking to imitate me. NO PRESSURE HERE! Perhaps Mother Teresa said it best when she stated, "Many people mistake our work for our vocation. Our vocation is the love of Jesus". Your work location should not be an excuse to relax your faith; instead, your work location should be a testimony to your gratitude for God's provision. My interactions with D.J. have been an unsolicited affirmation my vocation is not a vacation from my relationship with Jesus Christ.

And now for the reality check. I have spent several years living out the responsibilities of being blessed as a daddy. First was the birth of Melissa and then the addition of Rhonda. Pati and I have laughed, cried, worked, prayed, prayed, and prayed some more as we have lived out the many facets of the blessings of parenting. And yes, we have walked with the girls through some significant challenges. The importance of doing my best to Himitate is emphasized because the next generation is watching how I 'daddy' through stuff. My prayer every day is to represent Jesus well in all things. My only shot at getting remotely close to living out that prayer is to worship Him, seek His truth, and chat with Him, so I can Himitate.

Oops. I need to make a serious correction. I made the statement the next generation is watching. The truth is the next generations are watching. In a miraculous story of extravagant blessings, the next generations are now watching. I am observing this scenario of imitation play out as Rylee and Reed watch and repeat everything Bill and Rhonda say and do. And with the addition of Marielle Jo and Samuel, Melissa and Jens are loving and nurturing our Norwegian grandkids. Pati and I are affectionately called Gannma and Gannpa. It doesn't get much better than that. There is generational impact resting squarely on my shoulders so I must take my ability to Himitate very seriously as I may need one of these Gannkids to feed me some day.

If I Himitate well, my legacy will be all about Him and little to do with me. Just like the legacies of my mom and dad, I pray my legacy will be one that impacts the next generation(s) to do their best to imitate Jesus Christ. Himitate.

Him Still Changes Everything

Chapter 5 Himitate

Reflections

1. Who do you imitate?
2. In relation to the facets of life noted below who do you recognize as someone you should imitate?
    a. Family
    b. Marriage
    c. Parenting
    d. Career
    e. Community
    f. Church
    g. Relationships / Friendships
    h. Health
    i. Spare time
3. Pick three of the people identified in #2 and offer some reasons why you chose them.
4. A few years ago, there was a popular movement based on the question 'What Would Jesus Do' (WWJD). I must admit that even on my 'best' days, I come up short in regard to imitating Jesus. Knowing we will all fall short of Himitation, how intentional are you at **seeking to imitate** Him?

Your acceptance of Him.... Changes Everything

Chapter 6 Himbark

Embark – the act, process, or an instance of embarking; to commence a new project, or venture
Himbark – trusting in Him, when commencing or engaging in a new project or venture

I had been teaching 6th Grade Sunday School for several years and each year the story of Jonah would make my list of potential lessons. One particular year a dad approached me the Sunday after the class had learned about Jonah. His 13-year-old son had apparently been sharing what he had learned in my class and his dad had some questions for me. The dad's comment was a little concerning because I wasn't sure if his comment was sincere or if he was just messing with me. After some idle banter, a not-so-idle battle ensued as there was a convergence of opposing thought. His core issue was I had taught the Jonah lesson as an actual event. His opinion was the Jonah story was just that; just a story. He was rather adamant in his stance so I let him school me for a bit, and then he paused his rant long enough for me to share my thoughts about Jonah.

The lesson of Jonah may very well be a simple story. However, I believe if God, the Creator of all, including all life, oceans, little fish and big fish decides to use a big fish to redirect a man's attention, then I believe almighty God can do it. For me, I believe God is the Creator. I believe He parted the Red Sea. I believe He instructed Noah to build a big boat. I believe God sent His only begotten Son. I believe I have eternal life with Him because I believe Jesus Christ died on a cross for my sin, was buried, and ascended into heaven, and sits at the right hand of God the Father. I believe the Jonah event is true because, in comparison to the other miraculous events, Jonah's embarkation inside a big fish is relatively simple… for God.

Pati and I have embarked on some great vacations on big boats, however, prior to our first cruise I was a bit apprehensive. Several years ago we agreed to take a short three-day cruise out of Galveston. We had a fantastic time and I basically cried (sobbed) like a baby when I was forced to leave my new favorite place. I could have as much pizza and ice cream as I wanted, whenever I wanted it. I could stay in the shade and Pati could lay in the sun and have people bring her poolside beverages with little umbrellas. I could play ping pong, basketball, shuffleboard, eat more ice cream, enjoy great entertainment, watch the sunrise, watch the sunset, and eat more ice cream.

This new adventure had won me over and we immediately began planning our next cruise; no more silly three-day voyages; it was time to get serious and go for weeks or months! Pati and I have thoroughly enjoyed our cruises. In 2008, as a gift for graduating from Texas A&M, we decided to take Melissa and her friend Kate on a cruise. Pati and I were going to take a cruise to celebrate their achievement whether they went or not, but they agreed to join us.

In addition to the unlimited access to ice cream, the ports-of-call are also of great interest to me. Pati and I had decided to take Melissa and Kate with us to a National Park / Beach in Cancun which we had visited on a previous excursion. The weather was beautiful and we made our way from the ship to the line of taxis anxiously awaiting the hundreds of cruisers. We were escorted to a 3-T (tiny tiny taxi). Once I crammed my 6'3" frame in a space created for a 5'3" passenger and all three ladies were packed into the backseat, I provided our driver with the desired destination. The very popular location, recommended by our Cruise Director and familiar to both Pati and myself, did not seem to be the desired destination of our driver. He flipped down his sun visor and presented me with a laminated picture of what now appeared to be our destination.

He seemed friendly enough and I made the decision to embark (boldness or readiness in undertaking) on this exciting adventure, with all five of us flying down a nice highway in a 3-T. And then, without any notice, our driver veered off of the nice highway and turned abruptly onto a very narrow dirt path. This is about the time that all three of the ladies expressed a high level of concern. As our speed decreased significantly, I was able to make eye-contact with a few men displaying machetes on both sides of the 3-T (tiny tiny taxi.) Pati made it clear that my decision to embark on this excursion was a horrible mistake. I began to have visions of never seeing these ladies again and having my life come to an abrupt end. I was officially concerned, but I was packed in that tiny tiny taxi like a sardine. I physically could do nothing and my inability to speak my driver's language limited my ability to do anything except pray. I was becoming more anxious as we continued further and further down this dark jungle path of the unknown.

Thank you, Jesus! Similar to how Jonah felt as he was regurgitated onto the beach at Nineveh, we were thrust from the narrow dark path onto paradise; an absolutely beautiful, brand new, private beach with cabanas, palm trees, waiters, beautiful water, brand new restrooms, the works. My attitude changed quite abruptly from one of fear and trepidation to an attitude of, "why were y'all concerned; I had this under control the whole time." It was an unexpected magnificent end to a prayer-filled, frightening embarkation. My desire was for Pati, Melissa, and Kate to have a great day, but I was fearful as I had no control over the journey that I had initiated, with an unknown final destination. I needed to protect them throughout the journey, from beginning to end, but helplessness had been thrust upon me.

Embarkations that have an uncertain destination tend to be both exciting and frightening. And yet, even those embarkations that have a known destination can be laden with life-jolting potholes. See, I am wired to lead, protect and provide for my family which means I need to make good decisions, conquer the enemy and provide safe passage for my girls; wife, daughters, grandchildren, , sister, and mom.

On December 12, 2015, my mom's embarkation that began on May 23, 1934, ended as she took her final breath. Hospice had come in the night before and shared with me and my sister Gail, some thoughts on what we should expect. I knew my mom's final destination, an absolutely beautiful journey's end, yet I found myself on this dark, narrow path, wanting to protect my mom, my sister, and my family. But I had no control over this embarkation. Mom had made it clear, more than once, she was ready for her eternal destination with her heavenly Father, but even with her known destination, this dark journey of uncertainty as to how I could protect her, comfort her, heal her, was an embarkation (commencing of a new venture) I was ill-equipped for. Standing on opposite sides of mom's bed, Gail and I held mom's hands, prayed for her peace and comfort, and cried as mom continued to strain for enough strength to win the battle for one more life-sustaining breath.

During those precious hours, God blessed me with a replaying of the previous three years.

Mom's health had begun to decline and with broken hearts, Gail and I (mostly Gail) had to find a place where mom could receive care twenty-fours a day. God provided a good place for mom and then a brand-new facility opened within a few miles. As soon as she was accepted, we moved mom to Highland Meadows, a place I unashamedly refer to as heaven on earth. As I continued to revisit our previous three years, I realized that God had given me a precious gift. I had spent more time with mom over the last three years than I had the previous twenty years. We had laughed, drank hundreds of large diet Cokes with three real cherries from the Sonic, eaten hundreds of fried chicken tenders with lots of gravy, hundreds of white chocolate macadamia nut cookies, played checkers, watched the Texas Rangers, Dallas Cowboys, Dallas Mavericks, Dallas Stars, Texas Tech Red Raiders, Wheel of Fortune, and Family Feud.

The narrow dark path suddenly became clear. Please understand that the embarkation was difficult and broke my heart. But my desire to comfort, heal, and protect was graciously and mercifully released to Him. Thank you, Jesus for Himbarkation; those ventures and journeys that I look back on now and recognize the relational purpose in the relentless process. This same realization that Jonah must have had during his three-days of quiet time.

Trust me, I did not easily accept the relentless process of mom's declining health, nor did I have a clue as to why the final leg of mom's embarkation process had to be so difficult. Mom had been in and out of the hospital several times, and a few months prior to her passing, she had been admitted once again for pneumonia. Between her urinary tract infections, Parkinson's, dementia and episodes of memory loss due to her brain tumor, we were never sure of the mental condition we would encounter with mom, but without fail, she would almost always ask me about 'the book'. She knew I had been writing some thoughts but the idea of putting them in a book had not been fully, or even partially, developed. However, for some reason, it was a topic that mom would always ask about, no matter how aware she was of anything else. During one of our hospital visits while she was battling pneumonia, we were reminded of the accelerated pace of her declining health. The pneumonia was deep and she continued to weaken. But sometime during our visit, from out of nowhere, mom says, "How's your book?"

As we were driving home, Pati said, "When we get home, do whatever you need to do to print a book for your mom, because if she passes away before she sees your book, you will never forgive yourself." I put some finishing touches on the content and created a rather unimpressive cover and ordered twenty-five books with a rush on the shipment. The books arrived three days later.

That Sunday after church, Pati and I went to the hospital to see mom. Mom was awake when we got there, still hooked up to an IV and monitors for her vital signs. I walked in and started asking the normal questions of how are you feeling, can I get you anything, etc. We had been there for a while when once again, out of nowhere, Mom says, "how's the book?" I proudly handed her the very first printed copy of Him Changes Everything. Grasping the book with her skinny arthritic hands, she looked at the cover, looked at me, looked at the book, opened it to a random page, looked at the back cover, and then back at me.

It would just be silly for me to try to explain how proud I felt at that moment as my eyes filled with tears. I suspect she felt the same way. That emotional tsunami came to an abrupt halt when mom's sweet little nurse arrived to take her blood pressure. Mom held up my book to show the nurse and that's when the nurse attempted to take it from her. With the sweetness of an angel she says, "Ms. Betty, let go of the book so I can take your blood pressure." Well, mom has this look that I have seen for decades that says, without words, "I don't think so." That sweet little nurse attempted once again to remove the book from mom's hands but it became apparent, I would need to assist. So, with great confidence, I reached over and ATTEMPTED to take the book from my mom, but she had a death grip on Him Changes Everything. The sweet little nurse said she would come back later.

My mom held in her hands, a book that contained some stories of a life that has been changed by Him, for Him. I pray that as you choose to embark on new journeys or ventures, you will realize the relational purpose God has for you at this very moment, as you read this book. My mom was determined for her legacy of Himbarkation to impact your relationship with Jesus Christ. This is probably a good place to stop reading and just thank my mom for her life in Him.

I, unashamedly, declare I do not understand His ways, (remember Jonah?) yet I am confident Him Changes Everything would have remained an unfinished word doc, tucked away on my computer in a folder labeled 'Documents', with no commitment to Himbark. My wife was undeniably correct when she encouraged me to Himbark with Him Changes Everything. I will forever cherish the moment when my mom would not let go of the book, as it reflects her faith in never letting go of Him because she knew the message of Him, most assuredly, Changes Everything.

I have been known to profess my shallowness by saying something like, "Lord, I believe there is purpose in what I am going through, but if you wouldn't mind, could we bypass the trial and just get to the blessing?" However, I know that the appreciation of the mountaintop has a much greater value when you embrace the battles fought in the valley.

In the twelfth chapter of 2nd Corinthians, Paul tells the church in Corinth about this thorn in his flesh. He says, *"Three different times I begged the Lord to take it away. 9 Each time he said, "My grace is all you need. My power works best in weakness." So now I am glad to boast about my weaknesses so that the power of Christ can work through me. 10 That's why I take pleasure in my weaknesses, and in the insults, hardships, persecutions, and troubles that I suffer for Christ. For when I am weak, then I am strong."*

I have experienced trials where I prayed 'some' of what Paul writes in that scripture... Lord, take it away. As I reflect on those tough times, my level of Himmaturity is revealed each and every time. Even though I was deep in prayer-mode, not once on our off-road excursion through the machete cleared jungle path of Cancun did, I say, "Ladies, please relax, God's grace is all we need!" However, as my sister and I stood beside mom on her final journey down the path for life-sustaining breath, we sadly, yet victoriously knew we were covered in the blessed assurance that, as mom was taking her last breath on her eighty-one-year Himbarkation, that YES INDEED, God's grace was sufficient for mom, me and Gail.

As you read this book (and the first book,) I pray you will realize the relational purpose that God has for you. As you prayerfully and intentionally place Him first, you are aligning your daily embarkation of both known and unknown destinations, with His plan and your purpose. May you realize your journey is a Himbarkation, and your awareness of His purpose will be awakened and energized.

Him Still Changes Everything

Chapter 6 Himbark

Reflections

1. Reflecting on your most significant embarkations, how well did you trust Him, when commencing or engaging?
2. God wants to embark with you. From the very beginning to the very end, and every step throughout, consider His presence.
    a. Are you planning an embarkation that does not include Him?
    b. Have you already embarked on a journey that needs to engage, or reengage, Him?

Chapter 7 Himergency

> Emergency - a sudden, urgent, usually unexpected occurrence or occasion requiring immediate action.
> 2. A state, especially of need for help or relief, created by some unexpected event
>
> Himergency – a sudden, urgent, usually unexpected occurrence or occasion reflecting God's grace and mercy
> 2. A state, especially of need for God's help or relief, created by some unexpected event

Biblical 911 Dispatch Center
"911… what's your name?"
"Adam"
"What is your location, Adam"
"The Garden"
"OK Adam, what is the nature of your emergency"
"I'm not sure, but you know that tree …."

Biblical 911 Dispatch Center
"911… what's your name?"
"Moses"
"What is your location, Moses"
"Tending the flock for my father-in-law, Jethro, and I am in the wilderness at Mt. Sinai"
"OK Moses, what is the nature of your emergency?"
"There is a bush on fire."
"Did you say a brush fire?"
"No, a single bush is on fire"
"Please put the fire out. I will hold."
"It won't go out. It's just burning."
"OK… just watch it and it will burn out."
"No, it won't. And now it says it is God"
click

Biblical 911 Dispatch Center
"911... what's your name?"
"Moses"
"What is your location, Moses"
"I have led the Israelites out of Egypt and we made it to the Red Sea, but now the Egyptian Army is coming up behind us. Oh, never mind, the water has just parted."

Biblical 911 Dispatch Center
"911... what's your name?"
"Pharoah"
"What is your location, Pharoah?"
"We are chasing the Israelites and crossing the Red Sea and..."
"Hello...Pharoah? Hello...are you there?"

Biblical 911 Dispatch Center
"911... what's your name?"
"Bob"
"What is your location?"
"I live across the street from Noah"
"Really Bob? I have asked that you and your neighbors to please stop calling. Noah can build a big boat."
"We know, but now there are all these animals."

The bible is filled with events that fulfill the definition of an emergency; *a sudden, urgent, usually unexpected occurrence or occasion requiring immediate action. Or, a state, especially of need for help or relief, created by some unexpected event.*

Those events around Moses and Noah were certainly unexpected. Can you imagine standing with Moses as he realized God was most assuredly speaking to him through a burning bush? Chapter 3 of Exodus describes this burning bush encounter and describes the call upon Moses' life. Chapter 4 describes Moses' attempt at refusing to obey God. Moses did not disagree with God regarding the need to free the Israelites. It was a fantastic idea, but Moses was fairly confident that this seemingly impossible assignment ought to be offered to someone with greater speaking skills, notoriety, and confidence.

My goodness that sounds uncomfortably familiar!

And once again, try to visualize standing with Moses as he stood at the brink of a slaughter by the Egyptian army. Exodus 14 describes the setting.
9 The Egyptians chased after them with all the forces in Pharaoh's army—all his horses and chariots, his charioteers, and his troops. The Egyptians caught up with the people of Israel as they were camped beside the shore near Pi-hahiroth, across from Baal-zephon.
10 As Pharaoh approached, the people of Israel looked up and panicked when they saw the Egyptians overtaking them. They cried out to the LORD, 11 and they said to Moses, "Why did you bring us out here to die in the wilderness? Weren't there enough graves for us in Egypt? What have you done to us? Why did you make us leave Egypt? 12 Didn't we tell you this would happen while we were still in Egypt? We said, 'Leave us alone! Let us be slaves to the Egyptians. It's better to be a slave in Egypt than a corpse in the wilderness!'"
13 But Moses told the people, "Don't be afraid. Just stand still and watch the LORD rescue you today. The Egyptians you see today will never be seen again. 14 The LORD himself will fight for you. Just stay calm.15 Then the LORD said to Moses, "Why are you crying out to me? Tell the people to get moving! 16 Pick up your staff and raise your hand over the sea. Divide the water so the Israelites can walk through the middle of the sea on dry ground."

Personally (please don't judge me) I find verse 15 to be a bit humorous. The Lord said, "Moses, why are crying out to me?" I sense that Moses MAY have wanted to say something like, "Really? Really God? Is this really the right time for this question?" The truth is God did not need Moses to cry out to Him. God had provided direction and protection, and He appealed to Moses to trust Him.

And then there is Noah. Can you picture what Noah's life must have been like as he humbly stepped into the spotlight of humiliation as his obedience and trust required him to build a really big boat for no apparent reason? Unlike the dialog between Moses and God, Noah simply obeyed. There is not one reference to Noah having an ounce of doubt, fear, or uncertainty. God's direction was clear and specific. Noah's response was prompt and complete, without debate or negotiation.

Even though both men initially responded differently, they responded. Moses and Noah responded to the emergencies, supernatural acts of almighty God, by staying aligned with God. Those two men were completely reliant on God's provision in order to fulfill His call on their lives. The scriptures are filled with examples of people, who in the midst of an emergency, move. They move with a faith secured by reliance on Him.

Does your relationship with God reveal a faith Himpowered by Him to survive and thrive through life's emergencies?

Standing in the hallway just outside his room in ICU, which was filled with medical professionals, I heard someone yell, "CLEAR!" And then I watched as a line of trained medical staff had formed to take turns providing CPR on my brother-in-law, Doug. For several minutes the line continued to move as one after the other stepped up to do everything possible to keep Doug alive. Then I heard it again, "CLEAR!" And once again the CPR process continued.

The entire family was in the hall, praying for healing and life. After several more minutes the doctor came and spoke to the family, informing us that Doug had stabilized, but the prognosis was not good. The doctor explained everything he was going to do and why. With the doctor's prognosis, each one of us had to begin to process this unexpected, unfathomable event. Doug was strong as an ox (seriously), and stubborn as a mule (seriously). But, the thoughts began, what if Doug does not pull through? At approximately 8:00 PM on May 24, 2017, the heart of this big, strong man failed.

As I began to pray for appropriate words to share for his eulogy, the word 'clear', kept coming to mind. It was an emergency and Doug's heart needed to be shocked. There was a means in place to do it correctly and the process was extremely important. In order to keep others from receiving the electrical shock, 'clear' was ordered. Anywhere from 200 to 1,700 volts could be delivered in order to allow the heart rhythm to return to normal. "Clear" was ordered and everyone surrounding him had to step away in order for his heart to be revived.

I have a sense our spiritual emergencies are remarkably similar to our physical emergencies. In our most severe, life-threatening moments (physical and spiritual), we seek answers from well-meaning professionals, family, friends, counselors, pastors, Hallmark cards, daily devotionals, Google, Pinterest, Instagram, etc.... Unfortunately, in our best effort to regain a life-giving heartbeat, we can become overwhelmed with well-intentioned, imperfect purveyors of opinion. You may feel the need to yell 'CLEAR', or perhaps there are moments when you need to pray for God to 'CLEAR' for you.

There are those times in our lives when emergencies overwhelm us, and 'CLEAR' is required for God to do what we need Him to do. An adamant 'CLEAR' is necessary to free us from unhealthy distractions, unhealthy relationships, unhealthy career choices, unhealthy religion, and unhealthy focus on past failures. The great news is 'CLEAR' is exactly where God wants us so we will reach out to Him, unhindered by the confusion of unhealthy noise.

There are several scriptures giving us Christ-like permission to 'clear'.

"Jesus walked beside the Sea of Galilee... 'Come, follow me,' he said." (Mark 1:16)

"Very early in the morning, while it was still dark, Jesus got up, left the house and went off to a solitary place, where he prayed." (Mark 1:35)

"But Jesus often withdrew to lonely places and prayed." Luke 5:15-16

"Once again Jesus went out beside the lake." (Mark 2:13)

"One Sabbath Jesus was going through the grain fields, and his disciples walked along." (Mark 2:23)

"Jesus withdrew with his disciples to the lake, and a large crowd from Galilee followed." (Mark 3:7)

"Jesus went out to a mountain side to pray, and spent the night praying to God. When morning came, he called his disciples to him." (Luke 6:12-13. See also Mark 3:13)

"When Jesus heard [that John the Baptist had been beheaded], he withdrew by boat privately to a solitary place." (Matthew 14:13)

"Because so many people were coming and going that they did not even have a chance to eat, [Jesus] said to [his disciples], 'Come with me by yourselves to a quiet place and get some rest.' So they went away by themselves in a boat to a solitary place." (Mark 6:31-32)

"Jesus went on from there and walked beside the Sea of Galilee. And he went up on the mountain and sat down there." (Matthew 15:29, ESV)

I actually thought I had finished this chapter months earlier but yet, here we go with an unexpected occurrence, a need for help or relief, created by some unexpected event; an emergency. Sometimes the emergency is not particularly personal, however, it requires immediate attention. And then there are those times when the emergency is deeply personal. So personal, any attempt to cope with it is best defined as impossible.

On December 12, 2015, Gail and I were standing on opposite sides of our mom's hospital bed as mom took her last breath, ushering in her final port of Himbarkation (earlier chapter). My sister had always been an incredible consistent source of strength for me as we walked beside our mom. She was a warrior for faith, stubborn for rightness, many times too generous, glue for the family, and my dear dear friend. My sister was my friend, and oh God how I miss her.

Her health emergency was centered on a condition we had never heard of; amyloidosis. I am now fully aware of that ugly word. Gail's amyloidosis attacked her heart and even though the doctors offered a treatment program, there was apparently nothing they could do. In October, prior to all of the details surrounding her health had surfaced, and at a time when we did not know how dire this emergency was, my incredible wife took my sister on a short three-day cruise (Himbarkation). I might add, for some reason I was not invited.

When they returned from their cruise, Pati shared her concern about Gail's health and Pati's concern was regrettably correct. My sister's simple life, consumed with caring for everyone else, was being disrupted with a barrage of medications designed for pre-, during, and post-, chemotherapy treatments. Her greatest fear of being dependent on others was becoming her reality.

Even though we were not invited, Pati and I joined Gail for her doctors' visits so we could help keep track of the massive amounts of information from the entourage of medical professionals. During one of her doctor appointments prior to beginning this new regiment, the doctor stopped the medi-babble and looked straight at my sister. He paused for a moment and asked if she was OK with everything she was hearing. Without blinking or hesitation my sister patted the doctor's hand and said, "Doctor, Jesus Christ is my Lord and Savior, and He's got this." She did not need to ponder the question or ask for clarity. She was angry about the perceived 'burden' being placed on her family and friends, but she was not concerned, in the least with her well-being.

On December 30, 2017, sometime between midnight and 10 AM, Gail 'slept' from her earthly place to her heavenly peace. It seems after one final score update assuring her Pati and Melissa were beating me and Jens in a hotly contested game of canasta, Gail laid her head on her pillow, snuggled up under her comforter, and went home to be embraced by her Comforter. After several attempts to reach Gail the next morning, Pati called Krystal and within an hour, Krystal and Gail's best friends Rick and Sue went to Gail's home and found her in her bed. I'll never forget how Rick described Gail. There were no signs of struggle. No signs of pain. Just an indescribable peace.

Gail was right. There was no doubt her health was an emergency, but her faith in Him (Jesus Christ is my Lord and Savior and He's got this) is a gift to me and you, in the form of a Himergency. And that is exactly what I shared at her memorial service. I shared the story of the conversation I witnessed between Gail and the doctor, and that I believe there was purpose in my presence at that appointment. So I looked at each section of the sanctuary and offered them Gail's Gift of thriving in response to an emergency. Have you accepted Jesus Christ as your Lord and Savior? Gail wants you to!

I was an emotional mess before, during, and after Gail's service, so I do not remember all of them, but several people waited to thank me for sharing Gail's words of comfort.

We either have been, are currently, or will be challenged with emergencies. You know that sudden, urgent, usually unexpected occurrence or occasion requiring immediate action, or a state, especially of need for help or relief, created by some unexpected event.

I am thankful for Gail's example of how one's relationship with Him changes everything. Placing Him first, in every aspect of your life, especially emergencies, changes everything.

Biblical 911 Dispatch Center
"911... what's your name?"
"Sonny"
"OK Sonny, what is the nature of your emergency"
"I am a sinner"
"OK Sonny. That's a Himergency... and He's got this"

Chapter 7 Himergency

Reflections

1. Reflect on your emergencies and write down the ways in which God was there?
    a. People
    b. Prayer
    c. Peace
    d. Provision
    e. Other
2. You may struggle with a life emergency in which you do not, or did not, recognize any aspect of God's presence. Would you offer that emotion to Him right now through a prayer of healing for your soul? We do not understand His ways or His thoughts, but we do know that God is not a God of chaos, despair, and confusion; God is a God of unfailing love, grace, and mercy. Won't you pray that prayer?

Your worship of Him.... Changes Everything

Your obedience to Him.... Changes Everything

Chapter 8 Himprint

Imprint – to fix indelibly or permanently
Himprint - to fix indelibly or permanently by the blood of Jesus Christ

John 19:30 "*... it is finished.*"

Matthew 27 *As evening approached, Joseph, a rich man from Arimathea who had become a follower of Jesus,* [58] *went to Pilate and asked for Jesus' body. And Pilate issued an order to release it to him.* [59] *Joseph took the body and wrapped it in a long sheet of clean linen cloth.* [60] *He placed it in his own new tomb, which had been carved out of the rock. Then he rolled a great stone across the entrance and left.* [61] *Both Mary Magdalene and the other Mary were sitting across from the tomb and watching.*

Matthew 28:5-6 *Then the angel spoke to the women. "Don't be afraid!" he said. "I know you are looking for Jesus, who was crucified. He isn't here! He is risen from the dead, just as he said would happen.*

Jesus Christ died on the cross.
Jesus Christ was buried in a tomb.
Jesus Christ was resurrected.

Do you believe those statements about Jesus Christ? Because of those truths, your salvation is an imprint of God's unfailing love and grace. It is fixed indelibly. It is fixed permanently. Done.

And there is not one thing we can do to change it. It is immutable. We can deny it. We can simply acknowledge it. We can debate it. We can ignore it. We can argue about it. We can laugh at it. We can discount it. We can reject it. But we cannot change it! The Creator has sealed His creation with the indelible, permanent blood of Jesus Christ. It is His Himprint.

Do you have an imprint? I do, but we will get to mine in a minute. Some might argue that a tattoo is a pseudo imprint as it is almost permanent. I read recently that there is new laser technology that can remove a tattoo, but the process is timely and costly. Some of my favorite people have acquired tattoos. I'm not a tattoo guy. I grew up believing that tattoos were reserved for military, bikers, and gang members. I am none of those. I am not sure how but something has happened in the past few years making getting a tattoo, once taboo, popular for anybody and everybody. As a wedding officiant, I became well aware of the popularity of tattoos, especially with the bridal party. It was not the groom and his groomsmen that were proudly sporting the ink (I think that's what 'tatts' are called). It's the bride, her bridesmaids, moms, and grandmothers who are getting the ink. And they are not getting butterflies, college sorority letters and puppies.

I will never forget one in particular. I will call her Susie (not her real name). I had presented a high-quality reverent ceremony reflecting God's beautiful design for their marriage and genuine love from 1st Corinthians 13. The couple had also asked to incorporate the popular tradition of assembling the unity cross. It was a lovely ceremony and I was so proud to have them turn to their guest as I presented them as Mr. and Mrs. for the first time.

I'm sure I did not actually say this out loud, but in my mind, I said, "What the heck is that?" As Susie turned her back to me, this beautiful sweet bride exposed to me some sort of one-eyed fire-breathing, fang-toothed, forked tongue, creepy huge tattoo. I think the stupid thing actually winked at me. Susie and her new husband came back out for pictures with me and I was scared to go near her. I was impaired for weeks by the imprint covering her back.

However, an imprint is not limited to ink. I have a few imprints that are not ink related; they are permanent scars. One scar is on my ankle and permanently reminds me of running through a door. I was not inebriated. We were playing freeze tag in the house. You all know how horrifying it can be to be tagged and frozen, so I bolted 'out' the front door which had a sliding glass panel. I miscalculated the door release and went 'through' the door instead. I have a tiny scar on my chest reminding me not to play with ice picks. I have a scar on my knee from crashing my bike into the curb while riding with no hands. I probably have a scar on my brain from crashing my bike into the curb while riding with no hands.

Perhaps however, scars having the greatest impact are the scars imprinted on others. My dad had two scars providing some interesting stories and life lessons. The most apparent was about a four-inch jagged line that looked a lot like a lightning bolt. As scars go, this one was really cool. But, just like all scars, there is a narrative behind the imprint. During a weekend away from his army base in California, there was too much beer, too much machismo, and too much trash talk that resulted in a fight. My dad was the battalion boxing champ so I suspect the broken beer bottle was his adversary's attempt to protect himself. So the story goes, the guy ran at my dad and before the fool went down for the count he hit my dad in the shoulder with the broken beer bottle. Dad's scar was a reminder drinking too much alcohol leads to bad things.

The other scar was on dad's left hand at the base of his thumb. He and his older brother were fishing and a water moccasin bit dad's left hand. However, the scar was not from the snake bite. The scar was from the gash that dad's brother cut with his knife to suck out the poison. Dad always accused his brother of trying to cut off his thumb. Dad's scar was a reminder snakes are bad bad bad. I hate hate hate snakes.

It strikes me just how important it is to know the complete story. For instance, if someone was to start reading this book, beginning with this chapter, the statement I made earlier, "I have a tiny scar on my chest that reminds me not to play with ice picks," would not signify anything other than the obvious. The value of the imprint is diminished if you do not appreciate the cost, and you cannot appreciate the cost if you do not know the complete story.

So, what if someone starts reading the bible from John 20:26?

[26] Eight days later the disciples were together again, and this time Thomas was with them. The doors were locked; but suddenly, as before, Jesus was standing among them. "Peace be with you," he said. [27] Then he said to Thomas, "Put your finger here, and look at my hands. Put your hand into the wound in my side. Don't be faithless any longer. Believe!"

If you do not know the complete story, the purpose of the scarred hands and pierced side may not mean much to you. So let's pick the story up in Mark 15. Jesus has just been falsely charged and Pilate, the Roman governor, ordered his soldiers to flog and crucify Jesus.

Mark 15:15-24 He ordered Jesus flogged with a lead-tipped whip, then turned him over to the Roman soldiers to be crucified.[16] The soldiers took Jesus into the courtyard of the governor's headquarters (called the Praetorium) and called out the entire regiment.[17] They dressed him in a purple robe, and they wove thorn branches into a crown and put it on his head. [18] Then they saluted him and taunted, "Hail! King of the Jews!" [19] And they struck him on the head with a reed stick, spit on him, and dropped to their knees in mock worship. [20] When they were finally tired of mocking him, they took off the purple robe and put his own clothes on him again. Then they led him away to be crucified. [21] A passerby named Simon, who was from Cyrene,[b] was coming in from the countryside just then, and the soldiers forced him to carry Jesus' cross. (Simon was the father of Alexander and Rufus.) [22] And they brought Jesus to a place called Golgotha (which means "Place of the Skull"). [23] They offered him wine drugged with myrrh, but he refused it. [24] Then the soldiers nailed him to the cross.

The soldiers nailed him to the cross. These are the scars, imprints, on Jesus hands Thomas said he needed to see and touch so that he could believe that Jesus was alive.

John 19:34 describes how the imprint on Jesus side was created.

[34] *One of the soldiers, however, pierced his side with a spear, and immediately blood and water flowed out.*

The physical imprints from Jesus' crucifixion were real to Thomas, but only after he saw them and touched them. Unlike Thomas, I will not see or touch those imprints, yet I am truly thankful for the narrative. The simplicity of the physical proof Thomas needed provides clarity for our belief Jesus is alive.

Please do not let the previous sentence go unchecked. The purpose of this chapter is to make certain His imprints have caused you to consider for the first time, or reconsider again, who Jesus Christ is to you because of what He suffered for you. The scars of His crucifixion are real, and they really are for you, for real. If you are like Thomas and have this thought you can only believe in Jesus once you see and touch his scars, then now is the time to thank Thomas for doing that just for you.

The indelible blood that flowed from His permanent scars, are God's imprint on the world. His Himprint was, is, and always will be His purpose. His plan and purpose for His creation has not changed, is not changing and will not change.

Himprint - to fix indelibly or permanently by the blood of Jesus Christ

John 19:30 "... *it is finished.*"

1 Peter 2:24 says it best; *He personally carried our sins in his body on the cross so that we can be dead to sin and live for what is right. By his wounds (imprints) you are healed.*

In the Himmaturity chapter I talked about what happens when we get squeezed. The reality is whatever is inside will soon be identified. What is identified about you when you get squeezed? Is it anger? Is it blame? Is it fear? Is it shame? Is it forgiveness? Is it unfailing love? Is it grace? Is it mercy? Is it Him? My prayer is the squeeze of life will reveal a Himprint reminding me my identity is in Christ.

My dear friend Krish was speaking to a large group about motivation and leadership. At the end of his presentation a woman waited patiently for the crowd of people around Krish to depart so she could ask him a personal question. She said, "Based on some of what you shared I think you are a Christian." Without pause, Krish said, "If what I said did not reveal without a doubt that I am a Christian, I failed." I suspect the woman was trying to be politically correct because I have heard Krish speak hundreds (yes hundreds) of times and there is no doubt when Krish is squeezed, his identity in Jesus Christ is revealed. The Himprint of Krish is an unadulterated reflection of Him.

The Himprint of "By His wounds you are healed" and "It is finished" ought to be truths influencing the way I live my life and the way I live my life ought to leave a Himprint on others.

Chapter 8 Himprint

Reflections

1. How many imprints do you have? Describe them.
2. How many Himprints do you have? Describe them.
3. What are your thoughts regarding the last sentence of the chapter? The Himprint of "By His wounds you are healed" and "It is finished" ought to be truths that influence the way I live my life and the way I live my life ought to leave a Himprint on others.
4. All of your scars, emotional, physical, relational, and spiritual, are real and have left an imprint on you. Jesus scars are real and have left a Himprint on the world. Will you believe without having to see them or are you holding out like Thomas?

Your conversation with Him.... Changes Everything

Chapter 9 Himpart

> Impart – to make known; tell; relate; disclose
>
> Himpart – to make Jesus known; tell about Jesus; relate to Jesus; disclose Jesus to others

Well, as it turns out, 'Himpart' could be its own book. People simply have a need to impart. We need to tell, make known, relate and disclose. Parents, grandparents, sisters, cousins, aunts, uncles, neighbors, teachers, cross-walk guards, preachers, employers, employees, managers, assistant managers, spouses, kids, grandkids, coaches, etc.... I simply have an endless supply of imparters; people who need to tell me stuff.

I will unpack Himpart in this chapter, however I pray in my attempt to abbreviate the narrative I do not discount its Himportance.

Let's kick it off with a story from a period of time when coaches were imparting their vast knowledge upon me.

On your mark. Get set. Go.

I am going to be brutally honest with those of you who have the cute little 26.2 stickers on your cars, bikes, kids, t-shirts, tattoos, yard signs, and billboards. We are all so very proud of you. But I don't get it. I do not understand the mindset of running 26 miles 385 yards, for fun. My issue may result from growing up in Lubbock, Texas where it may be the only place on earth where the wind (and sand) blows in your face no matter which direction you run. Running was not fun for me so my coaches exploited the running track as a disciplinary tool. Being late to practice meant I had to run laps. Blaming my tardiness on someone else added a lap. Making errors during practice were counted and added to my lap-tab for after practice conditioning (discipline). Not being able to hear what the coach was trying to impart resulted in running laps. Seriously? After running laps for being late, blaming mom, and making an error, it was virtually impossible for me to hear anything except my heart beat pounding on my ear drums. I could see the coach's lips moving but I could not hear anything. Apparently, he was yelling at me because I may have taken a short-cut across the end of the field. How did he see that? I could barely see through my now sandblasted eyeballs. I could not hear or see but I had to run another lap. And Lord help me if I had passed out. Calling the paramedics meant more laps for causing a distraction during practice.

Understandably, being on the track team was not of interest to me, so why in the world did the coaches make me run track. Perhaps it was the vast experience I had accumulated from running in circles. Long distances were not my strength so running sprints became the next running game I had to play. Why? I was not fast and really could not care less about winning a 100-yard dash. I don't dash. However, my motivation became clear as I heard the coach say the first three finishers could take a water break and bathe their eyes. I believe there were twelve of us lined up on the goal line when the coach blew his whistle. Within two to three seconds, I was eating the dust of the other eleven who were taking this dash game way too serious. As I moseyed up to the finish line, thinking the worst thing that could happen was a delay in my eye-bath, I became aware the number of racers had simply been reduced to nine. Did the coach impart that information? I do not think so. The remaining group got to do the little dash game again and then again, until there were only three remaining participants. Me and two other speed demons.

The coaches needed to impart their knowledge and experience upon me so I could become a better athlete. The challenge? I was really only interested in playing the game. Conditioning, practicing, understanding the role of my teammates, and listening to coaches go on and on about the other team, all seemed to be a major waste of my time. I just wanted to be a starter, play the game and of course I wanted to win. Nobody wanted to win more than me. However, my preparation did not reflect my desire to win. I was less

than impressed with the coaches' need to impart their wisdom upon me so I excelled at being adequate.
What happened to the impartations of wisdom and experience my coaches had taught and demonstrated? Nothing! I heard the words. I rejected the truths. I did not accept the silly thought preparing to go into battle would require knowledge and effort.

Impartations are just part of life. Everyone, and I do mean everyone, has information they believe needs to be imparted. The sheer volume of impartations is overwhelming, so we must filter, file, process and respond to a tremendous amount of information. That's a challenge for me. I am a single input guy. In order for me to know for certain what someone (Pati) is telling me, I must tune out everything else. Pati is a multiple input gal so she can hear, filter, file and respond to multiple simultaneous streams of impartations. Understanding that little nugget of wisdom will help your marriage. Try this guys; next time you sense your wife may be speaking to you, stop what you are doing and look into her eyes, listening with great intent to hear every word. She will either begin to weep as she recognizes your sincere desire to hear every word of her impartation, or she will freak out and just walk off.

What is the purpose of the never-ending barrage of impartations from this endless supply of imparters? Is it gossip? Is it well intended or mean spirited? Is it useless or useful? Does it initiate worthy banter or does it just not matter? Is it fact or fiction? Is it necessary and true?

That is the question. And it has always been the question. Is the impartation necessary and true? If we know and trust the source of the information then we can determine its validity. But even then, the truth may be fuzzy due to a variety of factors. For instance, there may be a language barrier. I have recently been exposed to the Norwegian language and I have no doubt what my new family is imparting is necessary and true, but I have no idea what they are saying. For me to discern what's being said as truth, I need somebody to translate it for me. I must be willing to wait for the words to be translated before I attempt to respond. For instance, when I was told to eat some kransekake, I politely refused. I don't eat kransekake. I did not know what it was but I have a rule; if I can't say it, I can't eat it.

It's funny how my mind works. I trusted the people who were telling me how good this was. They assured me I needed to experience the kransekake. Yet, I did not believe them. My logic was simple; I have lived sixty years without it. The really silly part is even after I saw it, watched others standing in line to get their piece, and the joy they experienced once they received it, I was still a bit hesitant. As it turns out, kransekake is quite good. I like kransekake a lot. It is actually a tower cake that looks like a Christmas tree made out of chewy donuts. I am rather fond of chewy donuts.

Two weeks before Pati and I left for Norway and my future encounter with kransekake, our church held its annual presbytery service. Prior to attending Gateway I had never heard of a presbytery service. This was all new to me, and much like the kransekake, my first inclination was 'thanks, but no thanks.' The really silly part is even after I saw it, watched others standing in line to get their 'word', and the joy they experienced once they received it, I was still a bit hesitant. Does that statement sound familiar?

I have become a huge fan of the presbytery services. I love going to the service and experiencing the presence of the Holy Spirit as the gift of prophecy is imparted to the attendees by way of receiving a word from someone who has the gift of prophecy.

June 10, 2018 was a perfectly normal Sunday except for the joy of hosting my little buddy Rylee for a sleepover with Gannma and Gannpa. There was a slight quandary because I had also planned to attend the presbytery service that evening. I really wanted to hang out with Rylee, but Pati assured me I should go to the presbytery service. I suspect Pati had no interest in sharing Rylee with me, so her words of encouragement may have been sparked by selfish motives. So, I decided to change my shirt and go to the presbytery service. That's important to know because I was wearing a bright red polo shirt and I did not want to draw attention to me. Previous presbytery services revealed what appeared to me to be an overt desire of some folks to purposefully try to be noticed by wearing bright colors, sitting on the front rows, or the ends of rows. I don't blame them for wanting to get a 'word', but that was not for me. I just loved watching the Holy Spirit reveal a prophetic word through others, for others. I changed into a dull blue button-down shirt and found a seat in the middle of a row toward the back of the sanctuary. Amongst the other 2000 people in the sanctuary, I settled in, and began praying and meditating for the service. Our great friends, John and Sharmy, came to the service and were initially sitting a row behind me, but I invited them to join me. It's worth repeating there were approximately 2000 (that's correct two-thousand) people in the sanctuary.

I was not disappointed in how the service played out as the presbyters walked around the sanctuary calling on individuals; individuals whom they did not know and then imparting a 'word in due season'. Between presbytery encounters I turned to John and carried on some innocent dialog, possibly about our upcoming weekly racquetball match. He looked past me and said, "Preston is coming up the aisle." This is how the next few minutes played out.

Preston (one of the presbyters) was probably sixty feet from where I was sitting and he says, "There's a gentleman sitting right back here (pointing in my direction)." There were several gentlemen sitting in this area so I kept waiting for 'the gentleman' to stand. Preston proceeded to call **me** out. What? My mind started racing. I had changed my shirt and sat back here for a reason. Pick someone else. I just came to watch!

Following is the word-for-word impartation (Himpartation) I received from Preston:

"What's your name? Sonny, great to meet you. This is a man who got in a boat that had a hole in it, didn't have an oar and found a

way to keep moving and he kept moving forward. He shored up the hole in the boat. You didn't put the hole in it. You just inherited the boat that way. You didn't have an oar but you started out cupping your hands and you worked and you worked, and you worked. There was no wind and there was definitely no sail. But I want to share the picture very clearly I felt the Lord gave me. I believe you are stepping into a completely new season where God is stealing your boat from you. It's a divine robbery. If God steals, He is stealing your boat. That may be the wrong way to say it. But He is taking the boat that you have known for years and he is bringing in a sailboat the size you can't wrap your mind around. It's got not one, not two, but multiple sails, but the best part of the picture I saw was not the boat or the size, but the divine wind that is coming into these sails in a way that you have never felt before. Sonny, I saw the Lord taking this boat. You've been kind of a one zip code kind of guy in that boat, because when you've got a boat that has a hole, you never know when the gum is going to pop up. You made an oar out of sticks at one point and you've been a one zip code guy. Not anymore, not anymore. I'm not saying literally, but I'm saying the box you have been in is like a Lego compared to the landscape, the body of water that the Lord is putting you on and the wind is going to take you. You don't need a steering wheel in the sailboat. The wind is going to get you there and it is going to be easier, easier, and easier than it has ever been. Faithful man. Everybody watch this because this is going to be interesting to see where his boat goes. God Bless you Sonny."

I am humbled that the Holy Spirit directed Preston to me and gave him this prophetic impartation. I have prayerfully sought God for revelation. In the same manner the goodness of the kransekake was revealed, I am confident the goodness of the prophetic word will be revealed, in God's perfect timing. I do not know when or how, but I am ready, willing, and able to embark on the USS Impartation! Unlike my response to my coaches, I am preparing every day so I am disciplined, conditioned, and ready for this boat to sail.

For those who may be curious as to how I have accepted the impartation as truthful and now proclaimed my desire for revelation, perhaps I should share a little insight. I trust the source of the impartation and I am not referring to Preston. Preston does not know me. I trust the Holy Spirit. The Holy Spirit knows me. The Holy Spirit revealed a vision about God's plan for my life; Himpartation.

The truth of this impartation of a prophetic word was nothing less than miraculous. Processing the meaning and application of the Himpartation for my life has been fun, exciting, disappointing, frustrating, slow, and incredibly encouraging. There were elements of the 'word' that seemed almost too easy and clear. For instance, I believe the 'boat' that God stole from me was my corporate career. Just four months prior to the presbytery service, AT&T determined that I was no longer essential.

As I wrote this chapter, the remainder of the 'word' remained a mystery. A sailboat with many sails? Divine wind coming into the sails? One zip code guy...not anymore? What was meant by the landscape, body of water, directed by the wind? I like the part about easier, easier, and easier than it has ever been. So, what's next? I have this amazing blessing of Himpartation and now I could use another Himpartation to define the first one. Because it's from Him and for Him, perhaps I should ask Him.

My first, and logical step was to search the scriptures for the answers. I know the answers are in His truth, but my meditations of scripture referencing a landscape, body of water, or being directed by the wind, took me to scriptures that I do not care for. My vision of landscape had me wandering in the desert for forty years. My vision of the body of water had me cruising inside a big fish with Jonah. And then I meditated on the wind, and my vision was quickly drawn to the many scripture references of the wind causing strife. None of these visions were the least bit comforting.

Come on Lord! Really? As I finished typing the previous sentence I received an impartation from the Holy Spirit. He told me to reread the word I received through Preston and count the number of times the word 'comforting' was stated. *None*. I recognized how easy it is for me to fall back into the trap of excelling at being adequate. Just like my coaches saw something in me worth pushing for, God did not create me for adequacy. God created me, and you, for amazing. I challenge you to never accept the mindset that adequate defines God's plan for you. And, it may not be comfortable.

Let me share a few scriptures that apply the word, impart.

Romans 1:11,12 [11] I long to see you so that I may impart to you some spiritual gift to make you strong— [12] that is, that you and I may be mutually encouraged by each other's faith.

Ecclesiastes 12:9 Not only was the Teacher wise, but he also imparted knowledge to the people.

If I may be so bold, I pray you will allow me to speak similar words over you and you receive them as a Himpartation for this moment in time, wherever you are, as you read this. Please receive them in the name of Jesus Christ.

I long for you to read and receive these words so He may impart to you some spiritual gifts to make you strong— that is, that you will be encouraged to Himbark, pursuing His calling on your life, utilizing the gifts He has bestowed upon you. Listen for Himpartations as you worship, pray and study. Our Teacher is wise, and he imparts knowledge to the people. Amen

And that's the way it is with the truth of the gospel. We impart the truth of Jesus Christ because we know it is good. I pray that you will toss away your acceptance of being adequate and receive those words as encouragement to seek Him with tenacity for His amazing plan for your life.

If you prefer to receive impartations by means other than words, please receive this little treasure as an option. Proverbs 29:15 says,

A rod and a reprimand impart wisdom, but a child left undisciplined disgraces its mother. My mom may have had that scripture framed, hanging just above another beautiful scripture from Proverbs 13:24, *whoever spares the rod hates their children, but the one who loves their children is careful to discipline them.*

Let's just say I had a lot of love imparted upon my backside as mom did not spare the rod, belt, tree switch, ping pong paddle (it broke), boat oar (it did not break). The boat oar was a little extreme and a one-time event. I had actually thrown a ping pong paddle at my sister. Her cat-like reflexes prompted her to duck which allowed the air-born ping pong missile to whizz over her head and penetrate the sheetrock wall in the garage. One might think that I was lucky the ping pong paddle missed my sister's head, unfortunately, it probably looked like an ax sticking out of the wall which generated a lot of excitement. In one movement, my mom grabbed a ping pong paddle and leapt over the table like a ninja warrior, landing behind me swinging the paddle which struck the target (my backside) and broke. I suspect that just made her angrier and the next best swingable object within her reach was a boat oar, which as I stated earlier, imparted a lot of love. The majority of the story is true - except for the ninja action.

When I began writing this chapter, I was focused on the thought the spoken word or written word were the only vehicles utilized to impart. Based on the 'boat oar' impartation I received from mom, I recognized the certainty other senses were feasible instruments used to impart. Beyond seeing, hearing, and touching, is it possible the other two senses, smelling and tasting, might also be conduits for imparting?

Pati and I attended a worship service with Rhonda and Rylee and my senses came alive to receive a special Himpartation. As five-year-old Rylee saw Gannma and Gannpa walking into the sanctuary she ran to us. I saw a Himpartation. As I picked her up, she said, "I love you Gannpa". I heard a Himpartation. During the worship songs she stood on a chair between me and Gannma and held my hand. I felt a Himpartation. My son-in-law Bill, was serving in the café as a barista and the place was filled with the aroma of fresh brewed coffee. I smelled a Himpartation. No, the smell of coffee was not the Himpartation. The aroma of the coffee ushered in the reality that my son-in-law was serving Him; and that was the Himpartation. After the service and a brief rain storm, we all went to dinner. Salads, spaghetti and meatballs, and a pesto pasta, all tasted very good. While I sat there watching Gannma play with Reed, and Rhonda and Bill parenting Rylee, I thanked God for the Himpartation as we sat at the table enjoying the taste of our food. I was once again reminded of the blessing of faith-filled family. I saw it; I heard it; I felt it; I smelled it; I tasted it.

Thank you, Lord, for continuing to Himpart upon me the desire to Himpart - to make Jesus known to my family. My family is Himportant. My mom and dad made sure I knew Him so one day my children, and grandchildren would know Him. Lord, I pray you will give my family eyes to see, ears to hear, hands to touch, noses to smell, and tongues to taste and speak, your great grace, mercy, and unfailing love. Lord, I pray you will put Godly people in their lives, who will Himpart to them in the same way you have put Godly people in my life.

A quick shout-out to those who have, do, and will impart their life on me. Some were coaches and teachers who saw potential. Parents who showed me how family is supposed to be done. A wife who never doubts my love for her. Children who recognize I feel blessed they love Him best. Men and women who have encouraged me when I become discouraged. And a savior who still Himparts, which still changes everything.

I love that truth. The truth my Savior still Himparts, which still changes everything. And He does it in totality, not in part. God does not impart in part. When God created, He did not leave anything undone. When God created man and woman, He did not leave anything undone. God loved the whole world (not just part of it), so much he sent his one and only Son, that whoever (not a select few) believes in him shall not perish but have eternal life (not part-time, full-time eternity).

*Romans 10:9-13 If you declare with your mouth, "Jesus is Lord," and believe in your heart that God raised him from the dead, you will be saved. [10] For it is with your heart that you believe and are justified, and it is with your mouth that you profess your faith and are saved. [11] As Scripture says, "**Anyone** who believes in him will never be put to shame." [12] For there is no difference between Jew and Gentile—the same Lord is **Lord of all** and richly **blesses all** who call on him, [13] for, **"Everyone** who calls on the name of the Lord **will be saved.**"*

God's creation is complete. God's purpose is fulfilled through Jesus. God imparted Himself upon his creation so the world would know Him completely, receive Him completely, and worship Him completely. Himpartation.

John 14:6 Jesus answered, "I am the way and the truth and the life. No one comes to the Father except through me.

According to the scriptures, and it does not matter which translation your read, the only way to receive your God-given salvation is through the cross and empty tomb. There are teachings that like to dance around the truth and negotiate that a loving God should, could, and would offer other options. I have been challenged by those who question and doubt but I don't have the capacity to understand what Jesus said in John 14:6 to mean anything other than what He said. Perhaps that truth would be easier for folks to accept if Jesus had said it in the positive. I am the way the truth and the life. And **everyone** comes to the Father through me.

An impartation offering you a 'non-Jesus' eternity with God, is a lie of the enemy. I pray you will hear, see, feel, smell, and taste the lie and run like hell from hell. Impartations that twist God's truth are eternally condemning.

There is a fundamental truth needing to be shared as I begin to bring this chapter to the finish line. (I hope you do not feel as if you have been running laps against the wind) I can pontificate brilliantly, or speak simply, in an attempt to impart the Good News of Him, but if it is not received then the purpose of the impartation is worthless. It would be like tossing the football with someone who does not use their hands. I may throw a perfect spiral but if it just hits you in the face and falls to the ground, I did not accomplish anything more than busting your nose and getting blood on the end of a perfectly good football. Please do not yell at me. It is up to you to receive the pass. It is up to you to receive what I am burdened to impart, which is all about Him.

As you read these words, please receive them as purposed, for soul purpose, because the most profound impartation is the one that changes your life. It is the ultimate Himpartation. God imparted His Son upon the world. Joseph and Mary certainly questioned the impartation, but they received it. Every word Jesus spoke was to impart Himself. Every laceration left by the flogging, the crown of thorns that bloodied his face, the cruel brutality of the crucifixion, and the miracle of the empty tomb, were necessary so the Himpartation would be fulfilled. In our humanness we question, but in our faith we receive. God's desire for you to receive His unfailing love was made known through the cross and empty tomb.

Verse 30 of John 19 adds an exclamation point; "It is finished". I understand that proclamation to mean, it is finished. In Norwegian, det er ferdig. In Latin, Consummatum est. French, c'est fini. German, es ist fertig. Spanish, esta terminado. Telagu, adi mugisindi. Zulu, sekuphelile. Texan, it's done.

The language does not alter the truth. Jesus said, "It is finished." His purpose to Himpart himself is complete. He gave himself, in fullness, to die for the sin of this world. His resurrection is the Good News

Him Still Changes Everything

God loves His creation, preparing the Way for everlasting communion with you. Please receive it.

As I reflect on the complete gift of His amazing grace, undeserved mercy, and unfailing love, my eyes begin to sweat. I am profoundly aware of my inept commitment to walk in a fullness of faith. My 'in part' commitment reminds me of my ongoing compulsion to accept adequacy as an appropriate result. His sacrifice deserves more.

I am thankful for a loving God who knows my desire for Himpartations to encourage, challenge, and burden me to Himbark on His purpose for my life, even if it requires me to get on a boat with many sails headed to a zipcode His divine wind sends me. Those opportunities to Himpart – to make Jesus known; tell about Jesus; relate to Jesus; disclose Jesus to others, every moment of every day.

Psalm 26:2 Test me, LORD, and try me, examine my heart and my mind... so that I may Himpart.

Chapter 9 Himpart

Reflections

1. Have you received an impartation while reading this book? If so, pray about it, and share your thoughts with others, asking them for prayer support and input.
2. As you worship, study, and pray, God may Himpart a thought to you about someone else. Pray about how and when you should share your impartation. Always cover the impartation with unfailing love, grace, and mercy. Write down names and any 'words' you have received for encouraging others.

Your pursuit of Him.... Changes Everything

Your submission to Him.... Changes Everything

Chapter 10 Himponderable

Imponderable - not ponderable: incapable of being weighed or evaluated with exactness

Himponderable - not ponderable without faith in Him; Incapable of being weighed or evaluated with exactness without Him

This chapter belongs to Pati. The word for Pati's chapter is imponderable. I do not mean she is in some way imponderable, but the word is hers. September 29, 2018, Jonathan Bernis, CEO at Jewish Voice Ministries International was the guest preacher for our weekend services. Pati and I were walking to our car after church and began our typical post-message parking lot banter, sharing thoughts about the message. One of Jonathan Bernis' statements was there is a difference between the questions, "where have you come from" and "where have you been brought from"? When Pati asked me what I thought about the message, I told her I needed to ponder those two questions, "where have you come from" and "where have you been brought from" because they were ponderable. For some reason she came back with, "perhaps it's imponderable".

That's when the banter picked up some steam. I laughed and said, "imponderable is not even a real word." She disagreed and I just snickered at the silliness of the thought that 'imponderable' is a real word. I was tempted to raise the stakes of this little word game but then I remembered a previous lapse in judgement costing me a one carat diamond pendant. It is not necessary to spend a lot of time here, but it remains imponderable she came up with 'Thomas Jefferson' as the answer to a question that I had placed significant value on her not knowing. She now sports a very pretty one carat diamond pendant.

I am extremely fortunate this 'imponderable' examination did not include another potential costly wager. Pati grabbed her handy dandy phone and did a word search for imponderable. I was wrong again. It is imponderable to me to learn imponderable is a real word, but what a great word it is.

One of the best ways to determine if a word is a real word is to check for synonyms and imponderable does not disappoint. Here are a few imponderable synonyms; unknown, unquantifiable, incalculable, indeterminable, immeasurable, and mystery.

Simply based on the definition and its synonyms, imponderable may very well be the best word for describing God's unfailing love for you and me. It is imponderable. I'm a sinner who, by faith in Jesus Christ, am forgiven. I have finally come to the conclusion it does not matter how much pondering I do; the sacrificial love of Jesus Christ will remain imponderable.

Before we plunge into a deep examination of the biblical applications of 'imponderable', let's explore a lighter side. There are things in life that I consider imponderable. One such quandary is this 'free range' designation for cattle. I know it's supposed to provide an organically enhanced hamburger, but I think it is rude to let the cows roam free in heavenly meadows believing they are actually free. They are only free to roam and eat until they are well done! It ends just as poorly for them as it does for those in a feedlot.

Before I embark on this imponderable sad sad sad narrative, I am aware that there will be folks who read this and totally disagree. I am okay with that and love them anyway. While watching a news show recently, I was shocked as the reporter was describing a new trend in disclosing the sex of a baby. They just don't. They refer to the baby as a they-by. The baby is not a he or she; the baby is a 'they'. X?!!*&#&^ Seems the parents do not want to confuse the infant by establishing gender specific stereotyped babies. Seldom do I blurt out an expletive but there are those moments overwhelming my blurt-filter.

And for the benefit of those who think I am making this junk up; this statement is from an article I read regarding this trend.

"The going classification for babies has been pretty standard for the last 70 years or so — pink equals girl, blue equals boy. Not that associating color with a baby's gender is going to have much of an impact in the early days of their lives, but let's face it, it's hard to tell when they all have the same red, scrunchy face."

https://globalnews.ca/news/4152075/gender-neutral-baby/

I do not know anyone who looks at a newborn baby's red scrunchy face to find out if they just had a boy or girl. Did you just laugh out loud? I did, and then I wept. I wonder, is God laughing or weeping?

https://www.whattoexpect.com/pregnancy/fetal-development/fetal-sex-organs-reproductive-system/

I am not a doctor or scientist, but just for the sake of clarity let me offer a quote from www.whattoexpect.com regarding the physiological timeline for gender identity.
"Your baby's sex is determined at conception by his or her genes. Embryos with XY chromosomes become boys, and those with XX chromosomes become girls."

Plainly speaking, God created them male and female, and it is determined early on in the process of pleasurable procreation. It is imponderable to me as to why parents would not celebrate the birth of their baby boy or baby girl. I can't even imagine what our parents would have said if Pati and I had told them we just had their first 'grand-they-be'. I am quite confident my dad would have taken me back to the garage for another boxing lesson (that makes sense to those who read Him Changes Everything)

Perhaps one of the saddest and most disgusting headlines in the current culture (2024) is this absurd idea that the sex of a child can be changed.

If a 26-year-old man or woman decides to partake in the enemy's lie that a sex-change is what is needed for some sort of self-actualization, then that's on them. But as soon as a child is somehow affirmed that he or she should have a sex-change, it is time to stand in the gap and fight for the children to be exactly who God created them to be from their birth. Woven in their mother's womb. If the parents, teachers, counselors and other adults are encouraging the sex-change, please call CPS. It is imponderable that adults would approve and doctors are willing.

Here's a thought. The parent(s) should be required to undergo the same procedure they are endorsing for their child.

Lord, protect Your children and forgive us for the tolerance of evil.

Enough of this extremely dangerous nonsense.

Genesis 1:27 So God created human beings in his own image. In the image of God he created them; male and female he created them.

Genesis 5:2 He created them male and female, and he blessed them and called them "human."

God created man and woman for the purpose of family. God created marriage with Adam and Eve, man and woman, to be in a sacrificial loving relationship with each other and God, as a means for the family to procreate. And our loving God designed the process of procreation to be pleasurable between husband and wife. Thank you, God.

As I continued to ponder what I should offer as appropriate text concerning Himponderable, I became distracted by the sheer volume of biblical material. This is where some specific prayer was invoked. I could actually copy and paste the entire bible here, provide a link to bible websites, or just stop typing so you could stop reading this book and encourage you to open the pages of your own bible and start reading.

From the beginning in Genesis to the end in Revelations, we encounter the mystery of God and we attempt to examine and solve for logical human understanding. We can't. However, God gives us a little understanding as to why we can't understand. Isaiah 55:8 says,
"My thoughts are nothing like your thoughts," says the LORD. "And my ways are far beyond anything you could imagine.
I suppose it helps for me to know I cannot possibly know, or even imagine, God's thoughts or ways. Everything about Him is Himponderable and by faith, lives are transformed.

Something miraculous happened to Saul / Paul transforming the eradicator of Christians into the warrior for the truth of Jesus Christ. I wonder how Paul would answer those two questions.

Hey Paul, where did you come from? I was a Jewish native of Tarsus in Cilicia. I was brought up as a Pharisee and studied in Jerusalem. I opposed the Christian movement.

Hey Paul, where have you been brought from? I am a sinner who had an encounter with the risen Christ. I am a servant to the Good News, forgiveness and unfailing love of God.

Hey Sonny, where did you come from? I was born in Lubbock and have lived in the Dallas area since I was 13. I studied (not much) in a variety of venues of higher learning. I worked in corporate America for many many many years.

Hey Sonny, where have you been brought from? I am a sinner who had an encounter with the risen Jesus Christ. I am a servant to the Good News, forgiveness and unfailing love of God.

Himponderable - not ponderable without faith in Him: incapable of being weighed or evaluated with exactness without Him

Chapter 10 Himponderable

Reflections

1. How do you answer each of these questions? Is there a significant difference?
    a. Where have you come from?
    b. Where have you been brought from? (Or, what have you been brought out of?)
2. As it relates to our culture today, what do you consider imponderable? Why?
3. Tolerance and political correctness have become weapons of the enemy. Does my narrative regarding 'they-bies' reflect intolerance or is it politically incorrect?

Your alignment with Him.... Changes Everything

Your love of Him.... Changes Everything

Chapter 11 Himmobile

> Immobile – not moving; motionless; not able to move or be moved.
>
> Himmobile – moving; in motion; able to move and to be moved by Him, for Him, with Him

To say I married well is an understatement of immeasurable proportion. Pati is a very good example of God's grace. She is beautiful, smart, caring, God-centered, fun, forgiving, family-focused, a great cook, and detail oriented. Other than the God-centered descriptor, I would have to agree with the thought opposites attract. Along with her individual attributes she also has a great brother, Mark. Mark is the best man; seriously, he introduced me to Pati forty years ago and was the best man at our wedding, and today he continues to be the best man. Similar to me, Mark also married very well. He and Vicki are amazing parents (raised three amazing boys who have become terrific men of God). I am well aware family dynamics can sever family relationships, but God has blessed Pati and I with a great family-friendship with Mark and Vicki. They're just the best of the best.

During our annual beach retreat at my nephew Jason's (you may remember Jason from the Himpowered chapter in Him Changes Everything) Jamaica Beach house in Galveston, Pati, Mark, Vicki and I spent a few days reflecting on our forty-year journey. The vast majority of our time together was uplifting, but there was a moment during our time when all of our mutual love and admiration came to an abrupt standstill. I believe we were in our eighth game of canasta when Vicki tried to kill me. Mark and I, also known as the Big Red Machine in the global canasta community, had put a whooping on the girls. We were ahead 5 games to 2. I really do not know how they won two games, but I suppose I am glad they did.

There are a few contributing factors influencing this incident. Four people who are usually asleep before the ten o'clock news were up past midnight for the second straight night and had been partaking in large amounts of mind-altering sugar, in the form of brownies, Pati's homemade sin-namon rolls, candy, chips and hot sauce.

Mark and I had secured a substantial lead and after the hand had been played, my partner began to utter a loving conciliatory remark to Vicki. At that same moment I took a harmless drink of a flavored carbonated water. Unfortunately, at the very moment my mouth was filled with carbonated water, Vicki said "shut-up". In forty years, I have never heard Vicki say anything harsh or mean, so her timing to unload this unwarranted taunt was shocking. I needed to have an outburst worthy of the moment; however, I had a mouthful of carbonated water. A mouthful of water that needed to go somewhere was developing into a tsunami, expanding my cheeks to retain an unprecedented amount of pressure. Swallowing became impossible and spewing onto the card table would have been unprofessional. Something had to give as that carbonated water was looking for a portal to erupt. My eyes began to bulge, my ears began to pound, and my nostrils were abruptly becoming the path of least resistance. Fortunately, my brief moment of being rendered immobile was overcome by swift action as I bolted to the kitchen sink. As I concluded the expulsion of the carbonated water, regaining a normalized breathing pattern, I heard Mark say, "Hey, when you come back from the kitchen bring the M&M's."

The next day God blessed us with a beautiful day at the beach. We absorbed sunshine, enjoyed enough breeze to keep us comfortable, and strolled along in the cool ocean water. I would take a few steps and then stop to engage in dialog or just to watch the other beach folks play in the water and on the beach. I was amazed how quickly I would begin to sink into the sand as the ocean waves would move in and out. Within a few moments my ability to move required more effort. I was not immobile, but if I stayed there too long, I could have become immobilized and the folks closest to me would be unaware of my constraint. I looked normal from what they could see, but what they could not see was that I was slowly becoming immobile. Defined as, not able to move or be moved, the immobilizing effect of the normal activity of ocean waves was innocently beginning to ambush me. I was beginning to settle.

Standing in the ocean is not the only place where settling initiates immobility. Settling for the world's definition of success can immobilize your desire for significance. Engulfed by the all-powerful appeal for political correctness causes us to settle for the opinions of self-appointed, self-righteous pontificators of their truth, but not the truth. We have settled into a state of disordered tolerance to the point of immorality. We are stuck between the Rock and the hot place.

My personal experience for settling impacted my career and my faith. Regarding my career, I settled into a pattern revealing a reenactment of excelling at adequacy. This attitude was not reflected in the quality of my work. I always received excellent performance appraisals. I will never publicly blame any individual for my lack of upward mobility during the previous eighteen years of my career, but there were two leadership decisions made regarding my opportunities that rendered me immobile. I continued to perform well but I allowed my distrust of leadership to prevail and my attitude of excelling at being adequate was reflected in my attitude. Everything looked normal to my coworkers and supervisors, but underneath the surface of the daily operations I was settling for 'my comfortable job'. I became comfortable in my immobilized condition. My comfort distracted me from pursuing my potential.

Regarding my faith, I settled into a religious pattern focused on my 'good works'. My religious activity immobilized my worship of Him. Much like standing in the ocean, to everyone around me I looked just fine, but the impact of settling for kudos and 'attaboys' for my good works had distracted my worship of Him. I was performing good deeds but my motivation was driven by the potential tribute in the next church bulletin. Standing in the hallways of the church, receiving frequent recognition, was influencing me to settle, much like the waves of the ocean had caused me to settle. Distracted by the activity all around me, I had settled into a self-righteous rut, and I was quite comfortable in my rut. I decorated my rut with the good stuff so that my rut became my sanctuary.

Have you decorated your rut in such a way it no longer looks like a rut? Have you been immobilized by a rut trap? If you answered yes, do not be discouraged. In Genesis we read the story of Joseph being immobilized by his brothers.

Genesis 37: 18-25
18 *When Joseph's brothers saw him coming, they recognized him in the distance. As he approached, they made plans to kill*
him. 19 *"Here comes the dreamer!" they said.* 20 *"Come on, let's kill*
him and throw him into one of these cisterns. We can tell our father, 'A wild animal has eaten him.' Then we'll see what becomes of his dreams!"
21 *But when Reuben heard of their scheme, he came to Joseph's*
rescue. "Let's not kill him," he said. 22 *"Why should we shed any*
blood? Let's just throw him into this empty cistern here in the wilderness. Then he'll die without our laying a hand on him." Reuben was secretly planning to rescue Joseph and return him to his father.

23 *So when Joseph arrived, his brothers ripped off the beautiful robe*
he was wearing. 24 *Then they grabbed him and threw him into the*
cistern. Now the cistern was empty; there was no water in it. 25 *Then,*
just as they were sitting down to eat,

Sadly, I must admit every time I read those verses I have to laugh. Don't judge me, just hear me out. Joseph's brothers were scheming to get rid of him. Killing him was their first plan but Reuben changed their minds by saying they should just throw him into a cistern and let him die there in the wilderness. So, they did just that. They threw their brother Joseph into a cistern to die.

And then it says, *just as they were sitting down to eat...* Are you kidding me? They threw their little brother Joseph into a cistern to die, and decided to have a desert burger. By immobilizing Joseph, his brothers assumed they would not be bothered by his preposterous dreams. As the story gets played out, we are assured of the promise of the prophet Jeremiah delivered to the exiled people. In chapter 29, Jeremiah tells us, [10] *this is what the LORD says: "You will be in Babylon for seventy years. But then I will come and do for you all the good things I have promised, and I will bring you home again.* [11] *For I know the plans I have for you," says the LORD. "They are plans for good and not for disaster, to give you a future and a hope.* [12] *In those days when you pray, I will listen.* [13] *If you look for me wholeheartedly, you will find me.* [14] *I will be found by you," says the LORD. "I will end your captivity and restore your fortunes. I will gather you out of the nations where I sent you and will bring you home again to your own land."*

Joseph's brothers meant evil, but God had another plan. Joseph did not die but was sold to some traders who were headed to Egypt, where the rest of the story describes very well the Lord's plans He had for Joseph. God knew the plans He had for Joseph. They were plans for good that gave Joseph an amazing future. Joseph prayed and wholeheartedly looked to the Lord. Joseph's captivity ended and he was restored. Joseph was Himmobilized!

If you are feeling immobilized stop reading and pray to receive the promise of Jeremiah 29:11-14. If you need a dose of some New Testament truth, speak the words from Romans 8:38-39 as part of your prayer.

Romans 8:38-39
And I am convinced that nothing can ever separate us from God's love. Neither death nor life, neither angels nor demons, neither our fears for today nor our worries about tomorrow—not even the powers of hell can separate us from God's love. No power in the sky above or in the earth below—indeed, nothing in all creation will ever

be able to separate us from the love of God that is revealed in Christ Jesus our Lord.

Paraphrased for the purposes of this chapter... *And I am convinced that nothing can ever* **immobilize** *us from God's love. Neither death nor life, neither angels nor demons, neither our fears for today nor our worries about tomorrow—not even the powers of hell can* **immobilize** *us from God's love. No power in the sky above or in the earth below—indeed, nothing in all creation will ever be able to* **immobilize** *us from the love of God that is revealed in Christ Jesus our Lord* **who Himmobilizes.**

If you like the stories of the Bible as reference material but prefer personal testimony as confirmation of God's promise to Himmobilize and restore, then please continue reading.

I have provided pre-marriage counseling for several couples and there is an unfortunate reality that many couples have sadly 'settled' for each other for a variety of reasons. This reality is a tragedy impacting our family for several years.

Part 1 of a story with a very good ending.
Melissa had come out of a marriage where she settled for a decent guy that met all of my expectations of a son-in-law. Unfortunately, they were not great together. I liked the young man; however, he just was not the guy for Melissa. She had become immobile in life, just going through the motions of marriage because she was married to a good guy that met my expectations. There was no joy. I'm not sure what finally triggered her desire to have her life back but she determined to get a divorce. Finding herself alone and striving to somehow correct her previous decision she settled for a guy who was the exact opposite of her previous guy. The enemy will use desperation in much the same way the ocean uses the waves. Waves of desperation cause us to settle for relationships that are not healthy and immobilize us. Melissa settled for an unhealthy relationship lasting five years. Rendered immobile within her family

and faith, she settled for chaos and confusion. Waves of fear, shame, and guilt had joined forces to amass depression looking for a portal to erupt.

But God!!!!!! Thank you, Jesus. When her settled desperation reached the point she could no longer retain an unprecedented amount of pressure, she came home. Even though she had been immobilized by fear, shame and guilt, God said, "child, I am not done with you. Shake off the dust from your feet and go home."

Part 2 of a story with a very good ending.
Jens-Boye Hauge had settled for a relationship that looked and felt like "a right relationship" to build his future on. During that time, he was establishing his understanding of the foundation good enough to build a life upon. So, for five years Jens pursued a relationship, believing it was right or could be made right. After five years Jens decided to take the next step, even though he knew there was something missing. He had talked with the young lady several times during their five-year relationship about her faith and he needed to make certain she understood his. Jens was confident in relaying and sharing his past experiences as well as his ongoing experiences in regards to his personal walk with God. However, Jens felt he was facing an impenetrable wall of disbelief and lack of support for this very important attribute of his life. Jens knew that he could not settle with a non-believer. Conversations increasingly led to quarrels and an increasing shaking of the security and foundation of the relationship.

Armed with Christian hope and an enduring spirit, he still did not give up, until the lady broke off the relationship. Sometime later he could see the hand of God in this, knowing the right thing to do was to keep praying for God to introduce the partner God would bless Him with. He was certain life would be much healthier in a strengthening partnership than the shattered disunion that ended after five years of struggle. So Jens-Boye Hauge spent the next two and half years praying for his future bride, whomever and 'wherever' she might be.

Part 3 of a story with a very good ending.
Of the five years that Melissa was surviving in the wrong relationship in Lewisville, Texas, Jens was in the wrong relationship in Kongsberg, Norway for half of the time and single for the other half. During those same five years, God was actively preparing to shake them loose from the bondage of settling for less than what God desired for them. Melissa came home to regain her identity in Him. Jens kept praying for his future wife. Neither Jens nor Melissa had any idea that trusting their immobility to Him would be the beginning of some significant need for mobility. God has blessed the Gann and Hauge families with the reality He truly is the God of healing, redemption, and unfailing love. (If the Hallmark people need another movie plot, have them call me)

So Joseph's immobility, turned Himmobility, started in a pit. Melissa's immobility, turned Himmobility, started in a bad relationship. Jen's immobility, turned Himmobility, started in a bad relationship. My immobility, turned Himmobility, started in my career and my church. The apostle Paul had some experience being immobilized as well.

On his second missionary journey, Paul and Silas were traveling from city to city and were in Philippi when they were arrested. In Acts 16, verses 23 – 34, we read about an immobility to Himmobility that I pray, I never experience. I have visited prisons and I prefer to stay out of them, however, if I am ever incarcerated, I hope it is because of my bold faith in Him.

Paul had just called a demon out of a woman and her owners were irritated that their income would be negatively impacted because of this. So they complained to the Roman officials and both Paul and Silas were arrested.

They were severely beaten, and then they were thrown into prison. The jailer was ordered to make sure they didn't escape. 24 *So the jailer put them into the inner dungeon and clamped their feet in the stocks.*

[25] Around midnight Paul and Silas were praying and singing hymns
to God, and the other prisoners were listening. [26] Suddenly, there
was a massive earthquake, and the prison was shaken to its
foundations. All the doors immediately flew open, and the chains of
every prisoner fell off! [27] The jailer woke up to see the prison doors
wide open. He assumed the prisoners had escaped, so he drew his
sword to kill himself. [28] But Paul shouted to him, "Stop! Don't kill
yourself! We are all here!"
[29] The jailer called for lights and ran to the dungeon and fell down
trembling before Paul and Silas. [30] Then he brought them out and
asked, "Sirs, what must I do to be saved?"
[31] They replied, "Believe in the Lord Jesus and you will be saved,
along with everyone in your household." [32] And they shared the
word of the Lord with him and with all who lived in his
household. [33] Even at that hour of the night, the jailer cared for them
and washed their wounds. Then he and everyone in his household
were immediately baptized. [34] He brought them into his house and
set a meal before them, and he and his entire household rejoiced
because they all believed in God.

I know I will go through seasons of immobility due to a variety reasons. But God! My faith in Him assures me if I will continue to pray and sing hymns to Him, the walls and chains of immobility will be removed. Your faith in Him will always love you from immobility to Himmobility. When you realize the waves of life have caused you to settle for less than God's desire for you, pray for His plan, seek His plan, and stay aligned with His plan.

Him Still Changes Everything.

Chapter 11 Himmobile

Reflections

1. What or who, immobilizes you from pursuing your identity in Jesus Christ?
    a. Relationship
    b. Work
    c. Gossip
    d. Religion
    e. Health
    f. Finances
    g. Time
    h. Other
2. How does your attitude or thoughts perpetuate your immobility?
    a. Fear
    b. Guilt
    c. Shame
    d. Doubt
    e. Conceit
    f. Pride
    g. Laziness
    h. Jealousy
3. What are your thoughts regarding the statement, "there is purpose in the delay"?
4. What are your thoughts regarding the statement, "comfort can distract me from my purpose"?
5. Have you 'settled' in any part of your life, for less than what God desires for you?

Conclusion

As you have continued to read from the introduction to this conclusion, I hope you have recognized a fundamental truth intertwined throughout this book. God loves you! God sent His Son for you. God's Son died for your sin and was resurrected for your eternal salvation. God is not angry with you. God pursues you. God's grace is sufficient for you. God's mercy for you is undeniable. No matter where you are as you explored these pages, I pray that the words of this book have humbly, yet miraculously, Himparted a desire for transformation. The sole purpose of Him Still Changes Everything has the same foundational message as Him Changes Everything; the sole purpose of this book is specific to 'soul' purpose. Restated, the one and only purpose of this book is, with Godly intent, to impact who you are.

If you are already grounded in your faith in Jesus Christ, I simply pray that this book allows you to consider your very own Him stories.

If you are questioning your faith and wanting to know more about Jesus Christ, I pray you will find a local Bible teaching church to guide, encourage, and pray with you. The victory over death has already been taken care of at the cross. Your eternity depends on your choice.

If you are still considering your options, please please please know that God loves you. He did not send His Son to die for a select few; God sent His Son to die for the whole world, which includes you. I pray at this very moment you will sense a nudging, a Himpartation, to seek Him. Your eternity depends on your choice.

Thank you for reading Him Still Changes Everything. Let me know how putting Him first in every aspect of your life still changes everything.

Him Still Changes Everything

Himmediately ... begin every morning immediately inviting Him to be first in every aspect of your day.

Himpending ... during the day, ask Him to be a part of all impending activities:
- Meetings
- Commute
- Conversations / Communications
- Tasks
- Thoughts

Himpty ... at the end of the day empty yourself of concerns, give thanks for His presence throughout the day, and ask Him for good rest.

Him Still Changes Everything

Call To Action

There are areas in our lives that need to be transformed, and that transformation involves placing Him first. I pray that you will pray about those areas of your life and commit to placing Him first.

Make some notes below to reflect a personal prayer, inviting Him to change that area.

Personal relationship with Jesus
Family
Marriage
Children
Parents
Church / Ministry
Community
Career / Work
Finance
Health
Friends
Hobbies
Technology / Social Media

What are people saying about Him Still Changes Everything

Him Still Changes Everything is going to help many people understand more fully the character of God. People will laugh at times and be touched emotionally at others. Everyone will appreciate your casual style that is easy to read and digest. I particularly want to express my appreciation for your summary questions that capture the essence of each chapter. Definitely worth the read. Ted Hyde

Overall, Him Still Changes Everything is inspiring. It is obviously God-breathed, and I know He is proud. The introduction makes it personal, and you feel like you are just having a conversation with Sonny. The ending of the Himpaired chapter is POWERFUL, specifically the last paragraph: "be desperate for Jesus, be Himpaired." So good, and leaving readers with a clear charge to act. I also love the "Himmutable" chapter because rules are truly so ambiguous in today's world. The story about your sweet Mom on Himbark will be so relatable for many that have walked their parents out of this earthly home. If I had to pick, Himpart may be my favorite chapter. The presbytery story is one of my favorites, and your application to the readers is personal and real. Thank you for this. Katie Willis

Him Still Changes Everything is a thought-provoking book full of humor, transparency, creativity and truth. Sonny moves the reader through Biblical content that makes them think, process, and reflect on God's character and amazing power. By creatively using life experiences, Sonny offers the reader an opportunity to see Biblical principles and ways to apply them to their life. This book approaches Biblical TRUTH in an entertaining and creative way. I especially enjoyed the Reflection portion at the end of each chapter, which offers each reader a more personal takeaway. I highly recommend this book to anyone who wants to know God better or be reminded of how amazing He is, and how deeply He loves them. Cristie Penn

Sometimes praise for an author's work is bookended by knowledge of the effort and expectation for the effort. Sonny Gann exceeds both expectations and effort in his newest book Him Still Changes Everything. The unique phraseology of action axioms that allow scripture to be both a reference and a reputation in daily living is both refreshing and rejuvenating. The added dependence on "Him" is articulated with practicality and poignance. You will be better for reading this beautiful approach to the living word and a loving God.
Krish Dhanam Author and Speaker

I love Him Still Changes Everything. It demonstrated the incredible faithfulness of God in our imperfect lives. When we are weak, He is strong. I loved all the stories which we can all relate to. S. Anthony

As we get older there are some things that stay the same – God can and does change things in our lives, even if we don't recognize them. Sonny is one of the few people I know that recognizes God in the everyday things in life. This book is a way for us all to see God in the impossible, improbable and even the mundane aspects of life. I am honored to call Sonny friend and my brother in Christ. Enjoy the journey as you read through this, his second book and find Him Changing Everything in your own lives. Matt Bieri

About The Author

Native Texan, born in Lubbock, Texas and moved to Dallas in 1973. Married to Pati in 1981 and they have been blessed with two married daughters, Melissa and Rhonda and four grandkids Sonny received his Bachelor's Degree in Business Administration from Dallas Baptist University and his Master's Degree in Professional Counseling from Amberton University. He provides pre-marriage, marriage, and other counseling services as a Licensed Professional Counselor. On January 1, 2024 Sonny launched Trellis Christian Counseling, LLC., in Grapevine, Texas.
Currently serves at his church in a variety of ways. Previously held multiple ministry and church leadership roles including Chairman of the Leadership Board, Mission Committee Chair, President of the Men's Organization, and Certified Lay speaker and has been invited to speak at a variety of events, venues and churches. Served on mission teams in Mexico, Egypt, and India, as well as several ministry teams as part of Kairos Prison Ministries. A past Board Member of the Denton Area Emmaus Community, HangTime Lunch Mentoring, and MALA Ministries.

You may contact Sonny Gann through Trellis Christian Counseling, LLC
www.trellischristiancounseling.com

Your life with Him…. Changes Everything

Made in the USA
Monee, IL
10 February 2025

11744363R00075